Jesus Our Eucharistic Love

EUCHARISTIC LIFE
EXEMPLIFIED BY THE SAINTS

The Eucharistic Miracle of Lanciano

Jesus Our Eucharistic Love

*Eucharistic Life
Exemplified by the Saints*

by

Father Stefano M. Manelli, F.I.

JESUS, OUR EUCHARISTIC LOVE is a new, unabridged translation of the latest Italian edition of GESU, EUCARISTICO AMORE, (Frigento, Italy: Casa Mariana, 1973) as revised by the author.

This book was prepared for publication by Immaculate *Media*trix [http://www.marymediatrix.com], an apostolic group of the Mission of the Immaculate Mediatrix Movement, under the direction of the Franciscan Friars of the Immaculate, POB 3003, New Bedford, MA, 02741-3003, USA.

Fifth printing   2008   15,000 copies

Imprimatur: Most Rev. Sean Patrick O'Malley, O.F.M. Cap.
                  Bishop of Fall River, Massachusetts, USA
                  Solemnity of the Sacred Heart of Jesus
                  June 14, 1996

The *Imprimatur* is a declaration of the Roman Catholic Church that a work is free from error in matters of faith and morals; but in no way does it imply that she endorses the contents of the work.

ISBN: 1-60114-029-0

TABLE OF CONTENTS

"To be possessed by Jesus and to possess Him—
that is the perfect reign of Love,"
St. Peter Julian Eymard

Preface

"Devotion to the Eucharist," St. Pius X, the Pope of the Eucharist, said, "is the noblest of devotions, because it has God as its object. It is the most profitable for salvation, because it gives us the Author of Grace. It is the sweetest, because the Lord is Sweetness Itself."

Devotion to the Eucharist, together with devotion to the Blessed Mother, is a distinctive feature of Paradise. The Angels and Saints of heaven also practice them. "There is a school in heaven," the mystic, St. Gemma Galgani, used to say, "and there one has only to learn how to love. The school is in the Cenacle. The Teacher is Jesus. The subject taught is His Flesh and His Blood."

The Eucharist is Love Itself, identical with Jesus. Therefore, it is the Sacrament of Love, the Sacrament that overflows with charity. It indeed contains the true, living Jesus—the God who *"is Love"* (Jn. 4:8) and who loved us *"unto the end"* (Jn. 13:1).

All expressions of love, even the highest and the most profound, are verified in the Eucharist. Thus It is a Love that is crucified, a Love that unites, a Love that adores, a Love that contemplates, a Love that prays, a Love that delightfully satisfies.

The Eucharistic Jesus is the Love that is crucified in the most Holy Sacrifice of the Mass, in which He renews the immolation of Himself for us. In sacramental and spiritual Communion He is a Love that unites, making Himself one with the person who receives Him. He is a Love that adores in the holy tabernacle, where He is present as a holocaust of adoration to the Father. He is a Love that contemplates in His encounter with souls who love to be *"at His feet,"* like Mary of Bethany (Lk. 10:39). He is a Love that prays, *"always living to make intercession for us"* before the Father (Heb. 7:25). He is a Love that, in the heavenly exhilarations of nuptial union, delightfully satisfies His favored spouses, virgins of both sexes, whom He draws to Himself in an exclusive love, as He drew to Himself

St. John the Evangelist, the virgin Apostle and the only one who *"leaned on His breast"* in the Cenacle (Jn. 21:20).

"To be possessed by Jesus and to possess Him—that is the perfect reign of Love," wrote St. Peter Julian Eymard. The Eucharist achieves this in all who are pure of heart, approach the holy tabernacle, and unite themselves to Jesus in the Host with humility and love. In the Eucharist, Jesus sacrifices Himself for us, He gives Himself to us, He remains among us with infinite humility and love.

"For One in such a lofty position to stoop so low is a marvel that is staggering," exclaimed the Seraphic Father, St. Francis. "What sublime humility and humble sublimity, that the Lord of the universe, the Divine Son of God, should so humble Himself as to hide under the appearance of bread for our salvation! Behold the humble way of God, my brothers. Therefore, do not consider yourselves to be anything on your own account, so that you may be entirely acceptable to One who gives Himself fully to you."

And St. Alphonsus de' Liguori adds with his usual affectionate tenderness, "My Jesus! What a lovable contrivance this Holy Sacrament was—that You would hide under the appearance of bread to make Yourself loved and to be available for a visit by anyone who desires You!"

May some remembrance of the priest, who every day gives us Jesus, and of the Blessed Virgin Mary, Mother of Jesus our God—and of all priests—be included always in our affection toward the most Holy Sacrament; for the Eucharist, Our Lady, and the priest are inseparable, just as Jesus, Mary and St. John the Evangelist were inseparable on Calvary.

Let us learn all this in the school of the Saints. They lived in a manner that was ardent and sublime, as true seraphim of love for the Eucharist. These are the ones, as Vatican II declares (*Lumen Gentium*, n. 50), who are the "most safe path" to Jesus our Eucharistic Love.

Father Stefano Maria Manelli, F.I.

Translator's Note

It has been over fifteen years since an English version of this work first appeared. The English text, though giving not even two-thirds of the Italian original, has been a source of consolation and inspiration to countless believers and has brought many others to the faith.

This new, revised translation, correcting a number of errors in the former English version, corresponds exactly to the author's complete text, and alone enjoys his approbation. Former readers, as well as those making acquaintance with Fr. Stefano Maria Manelli's reflections on the mystery of the Eucharist for the first time, will find in this new edition a spur to love their Eucharistic Lord more and more.

Feast of the Annunciation, 1996

The Flesh of Christ Revealed
in the Eucharistic Miracle of Lanciano

Jesus in the Eucharist is Emmanuel, that is, "God with us"
(MT. 1:23).

Chapter I

O Divine Eucharist!

❧ Jesus in the Eucharist is God among us
❧ Knowing, loving, and living the Eucharist

Jesus in the Eucharist is God among us

When St. John Marie Vianney arrived at the remote little village of Ars, someone said to him sourly, "Here there is nothing to be done."

"Then, there is everything to be done," replied the Saint.

And he began immediately to act. What did he do? He rose at two o'clock in the morning and went to pray near the altar in the dark church. He recited the Divine Office, he made his meditation, and he prepared himself for Holy Mass. After the Holy Sacrifice, he made his thanksgiving. Then he remained at prayer until noon. He would be always kneeling on the floor without any support, with a Rosary in his hand and his eyes fixed on the tabernacle.

Things continued this way for a short time. Then he had to start changing his timetable; and things reached a point requiring radical changes in his program. The Eucharistic Jesus and the Blessed Virgin Mary, little by little, drew souls to that poor parish, until the Church did not seem big enough to contain the crowds, and the confessional of the holy Curé became swamped with endless lines of penitents. He was obliged to hear confessions for ten, fifteen, eighteen hours in a day!

How did such a transformation ever come about? There had been a poor Church, an altar long unused, an abandoned tabernacle, an ancient confessional, and a priest with no resources and little talent. How could such a wonderful change develop in that unknown village?

St. Pio at San Giovanni Rotondo

We can ask the same question today regarding San Giovanni Rotondo, a town on Mt. Gargano, Italy. Until a few decades ago it was an obscure, unknown place amid the rough crags of a promontory.

Today, San Giovanni Rotondo is a center of spiritual and cultural life and its reputation is international. Here, too, there had been an unpromising, sickly friar, an ancient, dilapidated little friary, a small neglected Church, with altar and tabernacle left ever alone to this poor friar, who wore out his beads and his hands in the untiring recitation of the Holy Rosary.

How did the change come about? What caused the wonderful transformation that came to Ars and to San Giovanni Rotondo, so that hundreds of thousands, and perhaps millions, of persons have come to these places from every part of the earth?

Only God could work such transformations using, according to His ways, *"the things that are not to bring to naught the things that are"* (1 COR. 1:28). It is all due to Him, to the divine and infinite power of the Eucharist, to the almighty force of attraction which radiates from every tabernacle, and which radiated from the tabernacles of Ars and San Giovanni Rotondo, reaching souls through the ministry of those two priests, true *"ministers of the tabernacle"* (HEB. 13:10) and *"dispensers of the mysteries of God"* (1 COR. 4:1).

The Emmanuel

Let us ask the question: What is the Eucharist? It is God with us. It is the Lord Jesus present in the tabernacles of our churches with His Body, Blood, Soul and Divinity. It is Jesus veiled under the appearance of bread, but really and physically present in the consecrated Host, so that He dwells in our midst, works within us and for us, and is at our disposal. The Eucharistic Jesus is the true Emmanuel, the *"God with us"* (MT. 1:23).

"The faith of the Church," Ven. Pope Pius XII teaches us, "is this: That one and identical is the Word of God and the Son of Mary who suffered on the Cross, who is present in the Eucharist, and who rules in Heaven."

The Eucharistic Jesus is here with us as a brother, as a friend, as spouse of our souls. He wishes to enter within us to be our Food for eternal life, our love, our support. He wants to make us part of His mystical Body in which He would redeem us and save us, and then take us into the kingdom of Heaven to settle us in an everlasting bliss of love.

With the Eucharist, God has truly given us everything. St. Augustine exclaimed: "Although God is all-powerful, He is unable to give more; though supremely wise, He knows not how to give more; though vastly rich, He has not more to give."

When St. Peter Julian Eymard came to Paris, he was lodged in a very poor house in which many necessities were lacking. But when someone complained and another took pity on him, the Saint would respond, "The Blessed Sacrament is there. That is all that I need." When persons would approach him to obtain graces, help and comfort, the Saint would respond, "You will find all in the Eucharist: the warm words you want to hear, the knowledge and the miracles you need—yes, even the miracles."

"What more do you want?"

To the Eucharist, then, we should go. To Jesus we should turn—to Jesus, who wishes to make Himself ours in order to make us His by rendering us "Godlike." "O Jesus, Food of strong souls," St. Gemma Galgani used to say, "strengthen me, purify me, make me godlike." Let us receive the Eucharist with a pure and ardent heart. That is what the saints have done.

It should never be too much trouble for us to grow familiar with this unspeakable Mystery. Meditation, study and reflection on the Eucharist should have an important place each day on our timetable. It will be the time of our day richest in blessings.

It will do good to our soul and body. One reads in the life of St. Pius X that one day, when he was the parish priest of Salzano, he went on a visit to a sick altar boy. At that very moment the doctor also arrived and asked the sick boy how he was. The boy answered that on that day he was feeling better because he had been able to give a little instruction on the Eucharist to a few other boys.

At this response the doctor exclaimed with overtones of ridicule, "Oh! That's nice. During my medical studies I never heard that a little Christian teaching could have such effects."

At this sour remark, the priest immediately intervened in defense of the youth and said to the doctor, "Oh, we see very well the effects of your science, doctor, and even a nearsighted person would see them well, too, because the cemetery is full of them…. But Christian doctrine fills up a place which only those who are intellectually shortsighted would not be able to see: Heaven!"

The Eucharist is the heavenly *"leaven"* (Mt. 13:33) which is capable of fermenting, in the human nature of every person, all spiritual and temporal goods. It is so great a good Itself that one cannot desire anything else greater. What, in fact, could one desire more, when within himself he has Jesus, living and real, the God-made-man, the Word made flesh and blood for our salvation and happiness?

On his deathbed St. Peter Julian Eymard gave this excellent reply to a religious who requested a final point for reflection: "I have nothing more to tell you. You already have the Eucharist. What more do you want?"

Knowing, Loving, Living The Eucharist

St. Peter Julian Eymard rightly said that "when a spark of the Eucharist is placed in a soul, a divine germ of life and of all the virtues is cast into that heart. This germ is sufficient of itself, so to say [to do much]."

In order to explore at least some of the immense riches stored up in the Mystery of the Eucharist, let us engage in a constant, unified exercise employing mind, heart and will.

An exercise of the mind

First, with the mind one meditates in an attentive, orderly way on the Eucharist. This may be done with books which lead us to personally uncover and deeply ponder this Mystery of Love. A simple little work rich in content is St. Alphonsus M. de' Liguori's *Visits to the Blessed Sacrament and to the Blessed Virgin Mary*. In addition, there are the two precious little works by St. Peter Julian Eymard entitled, *The Real Presence* and *Holy Communion*.

We should, above all, turn to the school of St. Peter Julian Eymard, who was unequalled as an Apostle of the Eucharist. His vocation and mission was to lead all Christians to the Eucharist, to such an extent that people finally called him "the Priest of the Blessed Sacrament!"

When he founded the Congregation of Priests of the Blessed Sacrament, he offered his life for the Eucharistic reign of Jesus. At that time he wrote these ardent words: "Here, dear Jesus, is my life. Behold me ready to eat stones and to die abandoned, just so that I may succeed in erecting a throne for Thee and giving Thee a family of friends, a nation of adorers."

If we but knew the gift of a God who is Love and who gives Himself to us as a Gift full of Love! "The Eucharist," said St. Bernard, "is that Love which surpasses all loves in Heaven and on earth." And St. Thomas Aquinas wrote: "The Eucharist is the Sacrament of Love: It signifies Love, It produces love."

A concrete instance which rivets our attention on this Love is the Eucharistic Miracle of Lanciano (in the province of Abruzzi, Italy). There one venerates a consecrated Host which was transformed into living Flesh and which has been preserved in this state for more than a thousand years. The most recent chemical analyses of a particle of this Host verified the fact: it is indeed a piece of flesh which is still living and which is a part of a human heart *(see Appendix I)*. The Eucharist is indeed all one Heart!

One day an Arabian prince, Abd-ed-Kader, while passing through a street of Marseille with a French official, saw a priest who was carrying Holy Viaticum to a dying man. The French official stopped, uncovered his head, and knelt. His friend asked him the reason for this gesture.

"I adore my God, whom the priest is carrying to a sick person," replied the good official.

"How is it possible," the prince said, "for you to believe that God who is so great, makes Himself so little and lets Himself go even to the homes of the poor? We Mohammedans have a much higher idea of God."

The official answered, "It is because you have only an idea of the greatness of God; but you do not know His Love."

That is the answer. In confirmation of this, St. Peter Eymard declares: "The Eucharist is the supreme proof of the love of Jesus. After this, there is nothing more but Heaven itself." Yet, how many of us Christians do not know the vast extent of the love contained in the Eucharist!

An exercise of the heart

Second, to explore the riches of the Eucharist, we use the heart. If every Christian must love Jesus Christ: *"If any man love not Our Lord Jesus Christ, let him be anathema."* (I COR. 16:22), love for the Eucharist must spring from the heart and be ever alive in us all.

Among all the saints, perhaps one of the greatest models is St. Peter Julian Eymard, in whom love for the Eucharist reached such an intensity as to transform itself into a love of madness. It is for this reason that he was called "the fool of the Blessed Sacrament."

Now even love needs exercise. The heart needs to be exercised to love the true God, to long for *"The Author of Life"* (ACTS 3:15).

Holy Communion represents the loftiest point of this exercise of love, whose consuming flames unite the heart of a creature and Jesus. St. Gemma Galgani could exclaim in this regard, "I can no longer avoid thinking of how, in the wonderful greatness of His Love, Jesus makes Himself perceptible and shows Himself to His lowliest creature in all the splendors of His Heart." And what may we say about the exercises of the heart of St. Gemma, who desired to be a "tent of love" in which she would keep Jesus always with her? She longed to have a "little place in the ciborium" to be able to stay always with Jesus. She asked to become "a flaming ball afire with love" for Jesus.

When St. Thérèse of the Child Jesus had become quite ill, she dragged herself with great effort to Church to receive Jesus. One morning, after Holy Communion, she was in her cell, exhausted. One of the sisters remarked that she should not exert herself so much. The Saint replied, "Oh, what are these sufferings to me in comparison with one daily Holy Communion!"—Something not permitted everywhere in her times. She ardently pleaded with Jesus: "Remain within me, as You do in the tabernacle. Do not ever withdraw Your presence from Your little host."

When St. Margaret Mary Alacoque left the world and consecrated herself to God in the cloister, she made a private vow and wrote it in her blood: "All for the Eucharist; nothing for me." It is useless to attempt to describe the Saint's burning love for the Eucharist. When she was not able to receive Holy Communion, she broke out in ardent expressions of love like these: "I have such a desire for Holy Communion that if I had to walk barefoot along a path of fire to obtain It, I would do so with unspeakable joy."

St. Catherine of Siena often said to her confessor: "Father, I am hungry. For the love of God give this soul her Food, her Lord in the Eucharist." She also confided: "When I am not able to receive my Lord, I go into the Church, and there I look at Him…I look at Him again…and this satisfies me."

During her long and painful illness, St. Bernadette one time expressed the happiness that she felt in times of sleeplessness, because then she was able to unite herself to Jesus in the Blessed Sacrament. Referring to a little golden monstrance that was depicted on the curtain about her bed, she said, "His visit gives me the desire and strength to offer myself as a sacrifice, when I feel all alone and in pain."

This is called the "exercise of the heart."

The exercise of the will

Third, to find the riches of the Eucharist, one should exercise the will. One must do this by bringing the divine lessons of the Eucharist into his life. What good would it be to discover the infinite worth of the Eucharist as we ponder It and seek to love It at Communion time, if we do not proceed to live It?

The Eucharist teaches a love that goes beyond telling. It teaches total self-sacrifice, and an unequalled lesson in humility and self-effacement. It teaches patience and unrestricted dedication. But what do we draw from all this? We surely ought to achieve something, if we but reflect how Jesus has loved us and still loves us with such great generosity *"even to the end"* (JN. 13:1).

If we feel frail, we need to turn to Him, to speak to Him and not tarry about asking His help and support, for He is the very One who said, *"Without Me you can do nothing"* (JN. 15:5), while with the Eucharist not only are we capable of everything, but we also obtain what should amaze and move us, that is, our identification with Jesus, as St. Augustine tells us: "It is not a case of us transforming Christ into ourselves, as we commonly do with food; but it is Jesus who transforms us into Himself."

First of all, let us go before Him: *"Come to Me…and I will refresh you"* (MT. 11:28). Let us often visit Him, entering a Church every time we can and pausing a little while before the tabernacle, and put both our heart and body before Him! The saints were constantly eager to make visits to Jesus in the Blessed Sacrament, to make Holy Hours of adoration, spiritual Communions, ejaculatory prayers and earnest acts of love that come from the heart. How much profit they gained from this and how much good they passed on!

One day in Turin a friend, who was his companion from the university, asked Bl. Peter George Frassati, "Let us go and take an appetizer." Peter George took advantage of the occasion and replied, indicating to his friend the nearby Church of St. Dominic, "Of course. Let us go and take it in that cafe." Entering the Church, they prayed for a little while near the tabernacle; when they approached the offering box, Peter George said, "Here is the appetizer." And from the pockets of the two youths came alms for the poor!

Thinking of the Eucharist during his sermon, St. John Chrysostom once asked, "How can we make of our bodies a host?" and gave this answer: "Let your eyes look at nothing evil, and you have offered a sacrifice; let not your tongue speak unbecoming words, and you have made an offering; let not your hand commit a sin, and you have offered a holocaust."

Just recall the eyes of St. Colette, which were always lowered and recollected in sweet modesty. Why? She once gave the answer: "I have filled my eyes with Jesus, upon whom I have gazed at the elevation of the Host at Holy Mass, and I do not wish to replace Him with another image."

Let us think of the edifying reserve of the saints in speaking, controlling well the tongue which had been consecrated by contact with the Body of Jesus.

Recall the good works which souls, filled with a love imparted by the Eucharist, have accomplished because Jesus communicated to them His own sentiments of love for all of our fellow men, especially those most in need. Thus St. Francis de Sales exhorted every soul to approach the Eucharist as much as possible, because "by adoring and partaking of His beauty, His goodness and His purity in this Divine Sacrament, you will become all beautiful, good and pure."

Can we not also exercise our wills thus? Let us learn from the saints and start imitating their good works.

Bl. Pio of Pietrelcina celebrates the Holy Sacrifice of the Mass

Jesus "has loved me and has sacrificed Himself for me"
(GAL. 2:20).

Chapter II

Jesus for me

✤ Holy Mass is the Sacrifice of the Cross
✤ Daily Holy Mass
✤ Active and Fruitful Participation
✤ Holy Mass and the Souls in Purgatory

Holy Mass is the Sacrifice of the Cross

Only in Heaven will we understand what a divine marvel the Holy Mass is. No matter how much effort we apply and no matter how holy and inspired we are, we can only stammer if we would explain this Divine Work, which surpasses men and angels.

One day St. Pio of Pietrelcina was asked, "Father, please explain the Holy Mass to us."

"My children," he replied, "how can I explain it to you? The Mass is infinite, like Jesus…Ask an Angel what a Mass is, and he will reply to you in truth, 'I understand that Mass is offered and why it is offered, but its value, its worth, are beyond my comprehension.' One Angel—a thousand angels—all of Heaven knows this and thinks like this."

The Altar is Calvary

St. Alphonsus de' Liguori went so far as to say, "God Himself cannot bring about an action holier and greater than the celebration of a Holy Mass." Why? Because Holy Mass can be said to be a synthesis summing up the Incarnation and Redemption; It contains the Birth, Passion and the Death of Jesus—mysteries which God accomplished for our sakes. The Second Vatican Council teaches that "at the Last Supper, the night in which He was betrayed, Jesus initiated the Eucharistic Sacrifice of His Body and Blood, in order to continue the Sacrifice of the Cross throughout the centuries until His return." (*Sacrosanctum Concilium*, n. 47).

Earlier, Ven. Pope Pius XII had also formulated this stupendous insight: "The altar on Golgotha is not different from the altar of our churches; even this is a mountain [like Mt. Golgotha] on which stands a cross and the One crucified, where the reconciliation between God and man takes place." St. Thomas Aquinas, in an enlightening passage, wrote, "The celebration of Holy Mass has the same value as the Death of Jesus on the Cross."

For this reason, St. Francis of Assisi said, "Man should tremble, the world should quake, all Heaven should be deeply moved when the Son of God appears on the altar in the hands of the priest." Indeed, since it renews the Sacrifice of Jesus' Passion and Death, the Holy Mass, taken alone, is great enough to restrain divine justice. "All the wrath and indignation of God yield before this offering," writes St. Albert the Great.

St. Teresa of Avila said to her daughters, "Without the Holy Mass what would become of us? All here below would perish, because that alone can hold back God's arm." Without it the Church certainly would not last and the world would become hopelessly lost. "Without the Mass, the earth would have already been destroyed by the sins of men many ages ago," teaches St. Alphonsus de' Liguori. "It would be easier for the world to survive without the sun than to do so without the Holy Mass," said St. Pio of Pietrelcina. He was echoing St. Leonard of Port Maurice, who had said, "I believe that if there were no Mass, the world would by now have sunk into the abyss under the weight of its wickedness. The Mass is the powerful support which sustains it."

Sublime graces

Wonderful are the saving effects which every Sacrifice of the Mass produces in the souls of those who participate. It obtains sorrow and pardon for sins. It lessens the temporal punishment due to sins. It weakens the influence of Satan and the untamed impulses of our flesh. It strengthens the bonds of our union in the Body of Christ. It protects us from danger and disaster. It shortens the punishment of Purgatory; and it obtains for us a higher degree of glory in Heaven. "No human tongue," said St. Lawrence Justinian, "can enumerate the favors that trace back to the Sacrifice of the Mass. The sinner is reconciled with God; the just man becomes more upright; sins are wiped away; vices are uprooted; virtue and merit increase; and the devil's schemes are frustrated."

And so St. Leonard of Port Maurice did not tire of exhorting the crowds which listened to him: "O you deluded people, what are you doing? Why do you not hasten to the churches to hear as many Masses as you can? Why do you not imitate the angels, who, when a Holy Mass is celebrated, come down in myriads from Paradise and take their stations about our altars in adoration to intercede for us?"

If it is true that we all have need of graces for this life and for the next, nothing can win them from God like the Holy Mass. St. Philip Neri used to say, "With prayer we ask graces from God; in the Holy Mass we constrain God to give them to us." The prayer offered during Holy Mass engages our whole priesthood, both the ministerial priesthood (even apart from that of the individual priest at the altar) and the common priesthood of all the faithful. In Holy Mass our prayer is united with Jesus' prayer of agony as He sacrifices Himself for us. In a special way during the Canon, which is the heart of the Mass, the prayer of all of us becomes also the prayer of Jesus, present amongst us. The two Mementoes of the Roman Canon, during which the living and the dead are remembered, are precious moments for us to present our petitions. And in those supreme moments when Jesus in the priest's hands undergoes His Passion and Death, we can beg also for our own needs and we can recommend both living and deceased persons who are dear to us. Let us take care to profit by this. The saints held this to be very important, and when they recommended themselves to the prayers of the priests, they asked them to remember them above all during the Canon.

It will be particularly at the hour of death that the Masses we have devoutly heard will bring us our greatest consolation and hope. One Mass heard during life will be more profitable than many

Masses heard by others in our behalf after our death. St. Joseph Cottolengo assures a holy death to whoever assists often at Holy Mass. St. John Bosco also considers it a sign of predestination to participate in many Masses.

Our Lord told St. Gertrude, "You may be sure that to someone who devoutly assists at the Holy Mass, I will send as many of My saints to comfort him and protect him during the last moments of his life as there will have been Masses which he has heard well." How consoling! The holy Curé of Ars correctly declared, "If we knew the value of the Holy Sacrifice of the Mass, how much greater effort we would put forth in order to assist at it!" And St. Peter Julian Eymard exhorted, "Know, O Christian, that the Mass is the holiest act of religion. You cannot do anything to glorify God more, nor profit your soul more, than by devoutly assisting at it, and assisting as often as possible."

The Angel counts the steps

For this reason we must consider ourselves fortunate every time we have an opportunity to attend a Holy Mass. In order not to lose the opportunity, we should never withhold ourselves because it might cost us some sacrifice, especially on Sundays and holydays; indeed, on those days one is gravely obligated to participate in Holy Mass and whoever does not do so commits a mortal sin (*Catechism of the Catholic Church*, n. 2181).

Let us remember that St. Maria Goretti would travel on foot 15 miles to and fro to go to Sunday Mass. We should think of Santina Campana, who went to Mass while she had a high fever. Think of St. Maximilian M. Kolbe, who offered Holy Mass when his health was in such a pitiful condition that one of his brothers in religion had to support him at the altar so that he would not fall. And how many times St. Pio of Pietrelcina celebrated Holy Mass while he was bleeding and had a fever!

When illnesses sometimes prevented the saints from taking part in Holy Mass, they united themselves at least spiritually to the priests who were celebrating Masses in all the churches of the world. This was what St. Bernadette, for example, did when she had to be confined to her bed for a long time. She would say to her fellow sisters: "Masses are being celebrated in different parts of the world every hour. I unite myself to all these Masses, especially during those nights when I cannot sleep."

In our own daily lives, we ought to rank the Holy Mass ahead of any other good; for, as St. Bernard says, "One merits more by devoutly assisting at a Holy Mass than by distributing all of his goods to the poor and traveling all over the world on pilgrimage." And it cannot be otherwise, because nothing in the world can have the infinite value of one Holy Mass. "Martyrdom is nothing," the holy Curé of Ars said, "in comparison with the Mass, because martyrdom is the sacrifice of man to God, whereas the Mass is the Sacrifice of God for man!"

All the more we ought to prefer Holy Mass to mere amusements that waste our time and bring no profit to our soul. St. Louis IX, King of France, attended several Masses every day. A minister of the government complained, remarking that he could better devote that time to the affairs of the kingdom. The holy king replied, "If I spent twice that time in amusements, like hunting, no one would have any objection."

Let us be generous and willingly make sacrifices so as not to lose so great a good. St. Augustine said to his Christians: "Every step one takes while traveling to hear Holy Mass is counted by an angel. One will be given a high reward for them by God in this life and in eternity." The Curé of Ars adds, "How happy is that guardian angel who accompanies a soul to Holy Mass!"

Daily Holy Mass

Once one realizes that Holy Mass has infinite worth, he is not surprised at the saints' eagerness and care to attend it every day, and even more often when they could.

One day St. Pio of Pietrelcina said to a penitent, "If men were to understand the value of the Holy Mass, for every Mass such crowds would come to church that police would be needed to keep order."

Perhaps we, too, belong to that great number of Christians who have not understood the value of Holy Mass, and for this reason we lack the zeal and fervor that encouraged and inspired the saints to attend Mass every day and even several times a day.

The hidden bell

St. Augustine has left us this praise of his mother, St. Monica: "She did not let a day pass without being present at the Divine Sacrifice before Your altar, O Lord." St. Francis of Assisi usually attended two Masses each day, and when he was sick he asked a friar who was a priest to celebrate Mass for him in his cell so that he would not be without Holy Mass. Every morning after celebrating Holy Mass, St. Thomas Aquinas served another Mass in thanksgiving.

The shepherd boy, St. Paschal Baylon, could not go to church to attend all the Masses he would have liked because he had to take the sheep to pasture. But every time he heard the church bells give the signal for Mass, he knelt on the grass among the sheep before a wooden cross he had made, and in this way he would, from afar, follow the priest as he offered the Divine Sacrifice. What an affectionate Saint, a true seraph of love for the Eucharist! On his deathbed he heard the bell for Holy Mass and had the strength to whisper to his brethren, "I am happy to unite to the Sacrifice of

Jesus the sacrifice of my poor life." And he died at the moment of the Consecration in the Mass!

When St. John Berchmanns was still a young boy, he would leave his house every day to go to church at the first break of dawn. Once his grandmother asked him why he would always leave so early. The holy youth responded, "To win blessings from God I serve three Masses before going to school."

St. Peter Julian Eymard, even while very young, found delight in serving Holy Mass. At that time his town had this custom: the boy who would serve Mass would be the one who, in the early morning, would pass through the town ringing a small bell for a quarter of an hour to alert the faithful. How many times little Peter Julian hid the small bell the evening before to make sure of being the one to serve Mass the next morning!

A mother of eight, St. Margaret, Queen of Scotland, went to Mass every day and brought her children with her. With motherly care she taught them to treasure a little missal which she chose to adorn with precious stones.

"Bad management of time"

Let us manage our affairs so well that we will not lack time for Holy Mass. Let us not say that we are too busy with chores, for which Jesus could remind us, *"Martha, Martha, thou art troubled about many things; but one thing alone is necessary"* (LK. 10:41–42).

When one really wants to, one finds time to attend Mass without failing in one's duties. St. Joseph Cottolengo recommended daily Mass for everybody: for teachers, nurses, laborers, doctors, parents. To those who objected that they did not have the time, he replied firmly: "Bad management! Bad economy of time!" And he knew this generally was the truth. If we but appreciated the infinite value of the Holy Mass, we would be very desirous of assisting and would try in every way to find the necessary time.

When St. Charles of Sezze went about Rome begging alms for his community, he would take time out to make visits to a church to attend additional Masses. It was at the moment of the elevation of the Host during one of these Masses that he received the dart of love into his heart.

Every morning St. Francis of Paola went to church, and he remained there to attend all the Masses which were celebrated. St. Aloysius Gonzaga, St. Alphonsus Rodriguez and St. Gerard Majella used to serve as many Masses as they could. (They did this with such devotion and edification that they attracted many of the faithful into church.)

Venerable Francis of the Child Jesus, a Carmelite, served ten Masses every day. If it happened that he had a few less to serve, he would say, "Today I have not had my full breakfast." And what can we say of St. Pio of Pietrelcina? St. Pio heard many Masses every day, and participated at them by reciting many Rosaries! The holy Curé of Ars was not mistaken when he said, "The Mass is the devotion of the saints."

"I would walk ten miles"

The same must be said of the love that holy priests have had for celebrating Mass. It was for them a terrible suffering to be unable to celebrate Mass. "When you hear that I cannot celebrate Mass any more, count me as dead," St. Francis Xavier Bianchi said to a brother religious.

St. John of the Cross made it clear that the greatest suffering he had during his ordeal of imprisonment was that of not being able to celebrate Mass nor receive Holy Communion for nine continuous months.

Obstacles and difficulties did not count for the saints when it was a question of not losing so excellent a good. For example, one day in the streets of Naples, St. Alphonsus de' Liguori suffered violent pains in the abdomen. The religious who accompanied him urged him to stop and take a sedative. But the Saint had not yet celebrated Mass and his prompt response was, "My dear brother, I would walk ten miles in this condition in order not to miss saying Holy Mass." And his sufferings would not move him to break the eucharistic fast which at that time was obligatory from midnight. He waited until the pain subsided a little, and then continued his walk to church and Mass.

The Capuchin, St. Lawrence of Brindisi, was once in a town of heretics. Since this town had no Catholic Church, he journeyed forty miles on foot to reach a chapel cared for by Catholics, in which he was able to celebrate Holy Mass. Not without reason he often said, "The Mass is my Heaven on earth."

St. Francis de Sales one time was staying in a Protestant town. To celebrate Holy Mass he had to go every morning before dawn to a Catholic parish church which was on the other side of a broad stream. During the autumn rains the stream rose more than usual and washed away the little bridge on which the Saint had been crossing. This did not discourage him. In the place where the bridge had been, he threw a large beam on which he was able to cross over. In winter, however, because of the ice and snow, there was serious danger of his slipping and falling into the water. The Saint then devised a procedure whereby he put himself astride the beam and maneuvered across on all fours, so that he might not miss his celebration of Holy Mass.

We will never succeed in sufficiently pondering that Mystery beyond description, the Holy Mass, which reproduces on our altars the Sacrifice of Calvary. Nor can we ever have too much devotion for this supreme marvel of divine love.

"Holy Mass," wrote St. Bonaventure, "is an achievement of God wherein He places before our view all the love He has borne us. It is, in a certain way, a combination of all the benefits bestowed upon us." Therefore St. John Bosco earnestly exhorts us: "Take great care to go to Holy Mass, even on weekdays; and for such a cause be willing to put up with some inconvenience. Thereby you will obtain every kind of blessing from the Lord."

ACTIVE AND FRUITFUL PARTICIPATION

The infinite greatness of the Holy Mass should enable us to understand the need of attentively and devoutly taking part in this Sacrifice of Jesus. Adoration, love and sorrow ought to have undisputed predominance among our sentiments.

In a very moving reflection, quoted with emphasis by Vatican II, Ven. Pope Pius XII described the state of mind with which one should take part in the Holy Mass: it should be "the state of mind that the Divine Redeemer had when He sacrificed Himself—the same humble spirit of submission—that is, of adoration, love, praise and thanksgiving to the great majesty of God, so that we reproduce in ourselves the condition of victimhood, the self-denial that follows the Gospel's teaching, by which of our own accord we make a willing sacrifice of penance, sorrow and expiation for our sins."

Let us ask ourselves seriously: is this the state of mind with which we participate at Holy Mass?

The Crucifix and the candles

True and active participation at Holy Mass is what makes us into sacrificial victims like Jesus. Such participation succeeds in "reproducing in us the pain-shared features of Jesus" (Pius XII), bestowing upon us "a companionship with Christ in His sufferings" and rendering us *conformable to His Death*" (PHIL. 3:10). All the rest is mere liturgical ceremony, external dress. St. Gregory the Great taught: "The Sacrifice of the Altar will be truly acceptable as a Victim offered in our behalf to God when we make ourselves into the Victim." As a reflection of this doctrine, in early Christian communities, the faithful, wearing penitential garbs and chanting the litany of the saints, went in procession to the altar for the celebration of Holy Mass, with the Pope presiding. If we would go to Mass in this spirit, we should want to make our own the sentiment St. Thomas the Apostle expressed when he said, *"Let us also go, that we may die with Him"* (JN. 11:16).

When St. Margaret Mary Alacoque attended Holy Mass and would gaze at the altar, she would never fail to glance at the Crucifix and the lighted candles. Why? It was to impress on her mind and heart two things: that the Crucifix should remind her of what Jesus had done for her; that the lighted candles recall what she must do for Jesus—that is, sacrifice herself and be consumed for Him and for souls.

Every day the King of France, St. Louis IX, would assist at Holy Mass on his knees, on the bare floor. One time a valet offered him a kneeler, but the king told him, "At Mass God offers Himself as a sacrifice, and when God sacrifices Himself, kings should kneel on the floor."

St. John Bosco recommended that young people participate at Holy Mass by following the method of St. Leonard of Port Maurice, who divided the sacrificial part of the Mass into three parts, whereby one meditates, first upon the Passion of Jesus (from the Offertory to the Elevation); second, upon our sins, the cause of the Passion and Death of Jesus (until Communion); and third, upon the resolution to live a pure and fervent life (from Communion to the end of Mass).

To be able to do this in the simplest and most fruitful way, it is enough to commit oneself to follow attentively the priest at the altar. In this way one overcomes more easily the distractions and boredom. (And on Sundays one should not go in search for—as some do—the shortest Mass, simply because they can hardly wait for Mass to end!)

One day the father of Guido of Fontgalland asked his son how one should occupy himself during Mass. "During Holy Mass," the holy youth replied, "our single occupation is to follow it. It is enough to read with the priest the prayers that he recites at the altar...."

It is the same reply that Pope St. Pius X gave to whomever wanted to know what prayers to recite during Holy Mass: "Follow the Mass, say the prayers of the Mass!"

Be like Our Lady on Calvary

The best example of participation at the Holy Sacrifice is given us at the foot of the Cross by the most Blessed Virgin Mary, St. John the Evangelist and St. Mary Magdalene with the pious women (Jn. 19:25). To assist at Mass is very much like being at Calvary. The Servant of God, Pope John Paul II, in a discourse to youth, made this simple, moving statement: "To go to Mass means to go to Calvary to meet Him, our Redeemer." A meeting of love and sorrow with Jesus Crucified—this is participation at Holy Mass.

St. Andrew of Avellino used to be moved to tears as he said, "One cannot separate the most Holy Eucharist from the Passion of Jesus."

One day a spiritual son asked St. Pio of Pietrelcina, "Father, how should we take part at Holy Mass?" St. Pio replied, "As Our Lady, St. John and the pious women did on Calvary—with love and compassion."

In a missal of one of his spiritual children St. Pio wrote: "In assisting at Holy Mass, concentrate intently on the tremendous Mystery which is taking place before your eyes, which is the Redemption and reconciliation of your soul with God." At another time he was asked, "Father, why is it that you weep so much during Mass?" "My daughter," replied St. Pio, "what are those few tears compared to what takes place at the altar? There should be torrents of tears!"

At another time someone said to him, "Father, how much you must suffer by standing on the bleeding wounds of your feet for the entire time of Mass!" St. Pio replied, "During Mass I am not standing, I am hanging." What a reply! The few words, "I am hanging," vividly and strongly express what it is to be *crucified with Christ*—of which St. Paul speaks (GAL. 2:19). It helps us distinguish a true and full participation in the Mass from an academic, vain, sometimes showy participation.

A little episode in the life of St. Benedict is very beautiful. One day during Holy Mass, as soon as the words "This is My Body" had been uttered, St. Benedict heard a response coming from the newly consecrated Host: "And also yours, Benedict!" True participation at Holy Mass should make us victims (hosts) in company with the Divine Victim.

St. Bernadette Soubirous once expressed this bit of wisdom to a new priest, "Remember that the priest at the altar is always Jesus Christ on the Cross." St. Peter of Alcantara vested for Holy Mass as though he were about to go up on Calvary. For, in fact, all the priestly vestments have reference to the Passion and Death of Jesus: the alb calls to mind the white tunic which Herod made Jesus wear to make a fool of Him; the cincture recalls the scourging of Jesus; the stole reminds us of the rough cords which bound Him; the tonsure suggests the crown of thorns; the chasuble, bearing the figure of a cross, symbolizes the Cross borne on Jesus' Shoulders.

"Father, forgive them!"

Those who have assisted at the Mass of St. Pio recall those fervent tears of his, and his earnest request that those present follow Holy Mass on their knees; they recall the impressive silence in which the Sacred Rite unfolded; they remember the distressing suffering which showed itself spontaneously on St. Pio's face when he pronounced with great effort the words of Consecration; they can think back on the awesome, impressive silence of the faithful who filled the church while St. Pio silently prayed several Rosaries for over an hour.

St. Pio's sentiment of sorrow during Holy Mass likens him to the other saints. His tears were like those of St. Francis of Assisi (who sometimes shed tears of blood), and those of St. Vincent Ferrer, St. Ignatius, St. Philip Neri, St. Lawrence of Brindisi (whose tears at times soaked seven handkerchiefs), St. Veronica Giuliani, St. Joseph of Cupertino, St. Alphonsus, St. Gemma Galgani. But, after all, how is it possible to remain indifferent before the Crucifixion and Death of Jesus? We shall certainly not be like the Apostles who slept at Gethsemane (Mt. 26:40–45), and much less like the soldiers who, at the foot of the Cross, played dice (Mt. 27:35–36), heedless of the atrocious death-agony of Jesus! (And yet, this is the distressing impression that we get today when seeing some so-called "rock" Masses, celebrated to the rhythm of guitars playing profane and cheap tunes, with women in indecent attire and youths wearing the strangest fashions. "Lord, forgive them!")

St. John Bosco was also saddened at the sight of many Christians who, when in church, were "voluntarily distracted, showing neither modesty, attention, nor respect, standing [at times for kneeling] and gazing here and there. They do not assist at the Divine Sacrifice like Mary and St. John, but are like the Jews—putting Jesus again on the Cross!"

Let us look to Our Lady and the saints and imitate them. Only by following them are we on that right road which *"has pleased God"* (1 Cor. 1:21).

HOLY MASS AND THE SOULS IN PURGATORY

Once we have left this world, there is nothing we should want done for ourselves as much as providing for the celebration of Holy Mass for our souls. The Holy Sacrifice of the Altar is the most powerful intercessory prayer. It surpasses every prayer, every penance and every good work. It should not be difficult for us to understand this, if we recall that the Sacrifice of the Mass is the same Sacrifice as that which Jesus offered on the Cross and which He now offers on the altar, with its infinite expiatory value. Our immolated Jesus is the true Victim satisfying, or *"propitiating, for our sins"* (1 JN 2:2), and His Divine Blood is *"poured out unto the remission of sins"* (MT. 26:28). Absolutely nothing can be equalled to Holy Mass, and the saving fruits of this Sacrifice can be extended to an unlimited number of souls.

"Every debt must be paid!"

Once during the celebration of Holy Mass in the Church of St. Paul at Tre Fontane near Rome, St. Bernard saw an unending stairway which led up to Heaven. By means of it very many angels ascended and descended, carrying from Purgatory to Paradise souls freed by the Sacrifice of Jesus—a Sacrifice renewed by priests on altars all over the world.

Hence on the occasion of the death of a relative, we should place much more importance in having Holy Masses celebrated and hearing them, than in selecting sprays of flowers, finding dark funeral attire, or arranging the funeral cortège. St. John Bosco said that the "Holy Sacrifice of the Mass" is what "benefits the poor souls in Purgatory; in fact, it is the most effective means of relieving those souls in their sufferings, of shortening the time of their exile and of bringing them sooner into the blessed kingdom."

Many apparitions have been reported about souls in Purgatory who came to ask the offering of St. Pio's Holy Mass for their deliverance from Purgatory. One day he celebrated Holy Mass for the father of one of his fellow friars. At the end of the Holy Sacrifice, St. Pio said to the friar, "This morning the soul of your father entered Heaven." The friar was very happy, but said, "Padre, my good father died thirty-two years ago." "My son," St. Pio replied, "before God every debt must be paid!" And it is Holy Mass which obtains for us a treasure of infinite value: the Body and Blood of Jesus, the *"unspotted Lamb"* (Rev. 5:12).

During a sermon one day, the holy Curé of Ars gave the example of a priest who, celebrating Mass for a deceased friend, after the Consecration prayed as follows, "Holy and Eternal Father, let us make an exchange. You possess the soul of my friend in Purgatory; I have the Body of Your Son in my hands. You liberate my friend for me, and I offer to You Your Son, with all the merits of His Passion and Death."

"Nothing else but Masses!"

Let us remember: all prayers and good works offered to God are good and commendable, but when we can, let us above all have Holy Masses celebrated (especially the Thirty Gregorian Masses) for departed souls who are dear to us.

In the life of Bl. Henry of Suso, we read that as a young man he made this agreement with a brother of his religious order: "Whichever one of us outlives the other, let him hasten the glory of the one who has passed into eternity with the celebration of one Holy Mass every week." The companion of Bl. Henry died first in a mission territory. Blessed Henry remembered his promise for a little while. Later, because he had been obliged to celebrate Masses for others, instead of the weekly Mass which he had promised his friend, he substituted prayers and penances. But his friend appeared to him in a vision, much distressed, and reproved him, "Your prayers and your penances are not sufficient for me. I need the Blood of Jesus." Indeed it is with the Blood of Jesus that we pay the debts of our sins (COL. 1:14).

When St. John of Avila was on his deathbed, his confreres asked him what he desired most after his death. The Saint promptly answered, "Masses…Masses…nothing else but Masses!"

Also, the great St. Jerome wrote that "for every Mass devoutly celebrated, many souls leave Purgatory and fly to Heaven." The same must be said for Holy Masses devoutly heard. St. Mary Magdalene de' Pazzi, the well-known Carmelite mystic, was in the habit of offering the Blood of Jesus in suffrage for the souls in Purgatory. In an ecstasy Jesus showed her that many souls in Purgatory indeed were liberated by the offering of the Precious Blood. St. Bernadette was also full of compassion for the souls in Purgatory, and would often say to her religious sisters: "I have heard Mass for the souls in Purgatory: nothing but the Precious Blood of Jesus applied for them can liberate them." Nor could it be otherwise. In fact, as St. Thomas Aquinas teaches, just one drop of that Blood [if duly applied], with Its infinite value, can save the whole universe from every guilt.

Let us, therefore, pray for the souls in Purgatory and free them from their pains by hearing many Holy Masses and having Masses celebrated. "All good works taken together," said the holy Curé of Ars, "cannot equal the value of one Holy Mass; because they are the works of men, whereas Holy Mass is the work of God."

Angels gird St. Thomas Aquinas with the virtue of continence

St. Thérèse of the Child Jesus

"He who eats My Flesh and drinks My Blood abides in Me and I in him" (JN. 6:57).

Chapter III

Jesus in me

HOLY COMMUNION: JESUS IS MINE

In Holy Communion Jesus gives Himself to me and becomes mine, all mine, in His Body, Blood, Soul and Divinity. One day St. Gemma Galgani said to Jesus with artless simplicity, "I am Your master."

With Communion, Jesus enters my heart and remains corporally present in me as long as the species (the appearance) of bread lasts; that is, for about 15 minutes. The Holy Fathers teach that during this time the angels surround me to continue to adore Jesus and love Him without interruption. "When Jesus is corporally present within us, the angels surround us as a guard of love," wrote St. Bernard.

He in me and I in Him

Perhaps we think too little about the sublimity of every Holy Communion. Yet St. Pius X said that "if the angels could envy, they would envy us for Holy Communion." And St. Madeleine Sophie Barat defined Holy Communion as "Paradise on earth."

All the saints have understood by experience the divine marvel of our meeting and our union with Jesus in the Eucharist. They have understood that a devout Holy Communion means being possessed by Him and possessing Him. *"He who eats My Flesh and drinks My Blood abides in Me and I in him"* (JN. 6:57). On one occasion St. Gemma Galgani wrote, "It is now night. Tomorrow morning is approaching, and then Jesus will possess me and I will possess Jesus." It is not possible to have a union of love which is deeper and more total: He in me and I in Him; the one in the other. What more could we want?

"You envy," said St. John Chrysostom, "the privilege of the woman who touched the vestments of Jesus, of the sinful woman who washed His feet with her tears, of the women of Galilee who had the happiness of following Him in His pilgrimages, of the Apostles and disciples who conversed with Him familiarly, of the people of the time who listened to the words of grace and salvation which came forth from His lips. You consider fortunate those who saw Him…. However, come to the altar and you will see Him, you will feel Him [when received in Communion], you will give Him holy kisses, you will wash Him with your tears, you will carry Him within you like Mary Most Holy."

For this reason the saints desired and longed for Holy Communion with ardent love; for example, St. Francis of Assisi, St. Catherine of Siena, St. Paschal Baylon, St. Veronica, St. Gerard, St. Margaret Mary Alacoque, St. Dominic Savio, St. Gemma Galgani…. It is pointless to continue, for one would need to list all the saints.

For example, one night St. Catherine of Genoa dreamed that the following day she would not be able to receive Holy Communion. The sorrow that she experienced was so great that she cried unceasingly, and when she woke up the next morning, she found that her face was all wet from the tears she shed in her dream.

St. Thérèse of the Child Jesus wrote a little Eucharistic poem, "Desires near the Tabernacle," in which, among other beautiful things, she said, "I would like to be the chalice and adore the Divine Blood therein. I can, however, in the Holy Sacrifice, gather Him in me every morning. My soul is therefore dearer to Jesus, it is more precious than vessels of gold." And how great was the happiness of that angelic Saint when, during an epidemic, daily Communion was given to her!

A day without the sun

St. Gemma Galgani one time was put to the test by a confessor who forbade her to receive Holy Communion. "O Father, Father," she wrote to her spiritual director, "today I went to Confession and the confessor has said that I must stop receiving Jesus. O my Father, my pen does not want to write any more, my hand trembles violently, I cry." O dear Saint! Truly a seraph all on fire with love for the Eucharistic Jesus.

For the angelic youth Aldo Marcozzi, a day without Holy Communion was a day without the sun. In the winter mornings his mother wanted him to take something hot before leaving for school. In doing so, however, he would not be able to receive Holy Communion (since in those times fasting was required from midnight, and not for only one hour as it is today). The holy youth would then say to his mother with sorrow: "Mother, you will have to render an account to God for the Communions that you do not let me receive!" Another time a companion asked him if he was not feeling well because he appeared a bit sad. "Today is a bad day for me," replied Aldo, "because I have not been able to receive Jesus."

Similarly, St. Gerard Majella, for a false slanderous report from which he did not wish to defend himself, was punished by being deprived of Holy Communion. The suffering of the Saint was such that one day he refused to go to serve Holy Mass for a priest who was visiting, "Because," he said, "on seeing Jesus in the Host in the hands of the priest, I might not conquer a temptation to snatch a Host from his hands." What a longing consumed this wonderful Saint! And what a rebuke for us who, perhaps, are able to receive Holy Communion daily with ease and do not. It is a sign that we lack the essential thing: love. And perhaps we are so in love with earthly pleasures that we can no longer appreciate the heavenly delights of union with Jesus in the Host.

"My son, how can you perceive the fragrance of Paradise which comes forth from the tabernacle?" asked St. Philip of a young man in love with the pleasures of the flesh, of dances and amusements. The joys of the Eucharist and the satisfaction of the senses are *"opposed to each other"* (GAL. 5:17), and the *"sensual man perceives not these things which are of the Spirit of God"* (1 Cor. 2:14)—that is, he knows not the wisdom which comes from God.

St. Philip Neri loved the Eucharist so much that, even when he was gravely ill, he received Holy Communion every day, and if Jesus was not brought to him very early in the morning, he became very upset and could not find any rest. "I have such a desire to receive Jesus," he exclaimed, "that I cannot have peace while I wait."

The same happened within our own time with Padre Pio of Pietrelcina; for only holy obedience could make him wait until 4 or 5 A.M. to celebrate Mass. Truly, the love of God is a *"devouring fire"* (Deut. 4:24).

Jesus unites me to all

When Jesus is mine, the whole Church rejoices: the Church in Heaven, in Purgatory and on earth. Who can express the joy the angels and saints feel at every Holy Communion worthily received? A new current of love enters Paradise and a new delight comes to the blessed spirits every time a creature unites himself devoutly to Jesus to possess Him and be possessed by Him. A Holy Communion is of much greater value than an ecstasy, a rapture or a vision. Holy Communion transports the whole of Paradise into my poor heart!

For the souls in Purgatory then, Holy Communion is one precious personal gift which they can receive from us. Who can tell how helpful Holy Communions are toward their liberation? One day St. Mary Magdalene de' Pazzi's dead father appeared to her and said that one hundred and seven Holy Communions were necessary for him to be able to leave Purgatory. When the last of the one hundred and seven was offered for him, the Saint saw her father ascend into Heaven.

St. Bonaventure made himself an apostle of this truth and spoke about it in vibrant tones: "O Christian souls, do you wish to prove your true love towards your dead? Do you wish to send them a most precious help and golden key to Heaven? Receive Holy Communion often for the repose of their souls."

Finally, let us reflect that in Holy Communion we unite ourselves not only to Jesus but also to all the members of the Mystical Body of Christ, especially to the souls most dear to Jesus and most dear to our heart. *"Because the Bread is one,"* writes St. Paul, *"we, though many, are one body, all of us who partake of the one Bread"* (1 COR. 10:17). It is in Holy Communion that we realize fully the words of Jesus, *"I in them...that they may be perfect in unity"* (JN. 17:23). The Eucharist renders us one, even among ourselves, His members, *"all one in Jesus"* as St. Paul says (GAL. 3:28). Holy Communion is indeed pure love of God and neighbor. It is the true "feast of love," as St. Gemma Galgani said. And in this "feast of love" the soul in love can exult singing with St. John of the Cross, "Mine are the heavens and mine is the earth. Mine are men; the just are mine and sinners are mine. The angels are mine, and also the Mother of God—all things are mine. God Himself is mine and for me, because Christ is mine and all for me."

THE PURITY OF SOUL NECESSARY FOR HOLY COMMUNION

What is there to say about the great purity of soul with which the saints managed to receive the Bread of angels? We know that they had a great delicacy of conscience which was truly angelic. Aware of their own wretchedness, they tried to present themselves to Jesus *"holy and immaculate"* (EPH. 1:4), repeating with the publican, *"O God, be merciful to me a sinner"* (LK. 18:13), and having recourse with great care to the cleansing of Confession.

"Approach the Sacred Banquet," said St. John Baptist de La Salle, "with the same dispositions that you would desire to have in order to enter Heaven. One should not have less respect in receiving Jesus than in being received by Him."

When St. Jerome was brought Holy Viaticum at the end of his life, the Saint prostrated himself on the ground in adoration, and he was heard to repeat with profound humility the words of St. Elizabeth and those of St. Peter, *"How is this, that my Lord should come to me?" "Depart from me, for I am a sinful man, O Lord"* (Lк. 1:43; 5:8). And how many times was the angelic and seraphic St. Gemma tempted not to receive Holy Communion, considering herself to be nothing else than a vile "dunghill?"

They went to confession every day

St. Pio of Pietrelcina used to repeat with trepidation to his brethren, "God sees stains even in the angels. What must He see in me!" For this reason he was very diligent in making his sacramental Confessions. So too St. Teresa of Jesus, when she was aware of having committed the least venial sin, would never receive Holy Communion without first going to Confession.

"Oh, if we could only understand who is that God whom we receive in Holy Communion, then what purity of heart we would bring to Him!" exclaimed St. Mary Magdalene de' Pazzi.

For this reason St. Hugh, St. Thomas Aquinas, St. Francis de Sales, St. Ignatius, St. Charles Borromeo, St. Francis Borgia, St. Louis Bertrand, St. Joseph of Cupertino, St. Leonard of Port Maurice and many other saints went to Confession every day before celebrating Holy Mass.

St. Camillus de Lellis never celebrated Holy Mass without first going to Confession, because he wanted at least "to dust off" his soul. Once at sundown in a public square in Livorno, before taking leave of a priest of the same religious order, foreseeing that he would not have a priest to confess to on the following morning before his Mass, the Saint paused, took off his hat, made the sign of the Cross and went to Confession right there in the square to his confrere.

St. Alphonsus, St. Joseph Cafasso, St. John Bosco, St. Pius X, and St. Pio of Pietrelcina also went to Confession very often. And why did St. Pius X wish to lower the age for first Holy Communion to seven years, if not to allow Jesus to enter into the innocent hearts of children, which are so similar to angels? And why was St. Pio so delighted when they brought him children five years old who were prepared for first Holy Communion? St. John Bosco held that "when a child knows how to distinguish between ordinary bread and the Eucharistic Bread and is sufficiently instructed, one should not be too worried about his age. We should want the King of Heaven to come and reign in his soul."

Self-examination, repentance, purification

The saints applied to perfection the directive of the Holy Spirit: *"Let everyone first examine himself, and then eat of that Bread and drink of that Chalice; because he who eats and drinks unworthily, eats and drinks unto his own condemnation"* (1 COR. 11:28–29).

To examine themselves, to repent, to accuse themselves in Confession and to ask pardon of God, profitting even every day from the Sacrament of Confession, was something natural for the saints. How fortunate they were to be capable of so much! The fruits of sanctification were constant and abundant because the pure soul who welcomes into herself Jesus, *"the Wheat of the elect"* (ZACH. 9:17) is like the *"good ground…which bears fruit in patience"* (LK. 8:15).

St. Anthony Mary Claret illustrates this fact very well: "When we go to Holy Communion, all of us receive the same Lord Jesus, but not all receive the same grace nor are the same effects produced in all. This comes from our greater or lesser disposition. To explain this fact, I will take an example from nature. Consider the process of grafting: the greater the similarity of one plant to the other, the better the graft will succeed. In the same way, the more resemblance there is between the person who goes to Communion and Jesus, so much the better will the fruits of Holy Communion be." The

Sacrament of Confession is in fact the excellent means whereby the similarity between the soul and Jesus is restored.

For this reason St. Francis de Sales taught his spiritual children, "Go to Confession with humility and devotion…if it is possible, every time you feel in your conscience any remorse of mortal sin."

Sacrilege—a horrible sin

In this regard it is well to recall the teaching of the Church.

Holy Communion must be received only when one is in the grace of God. Therefore, when one has committed a mortal sin, even if one has repented of it and has a great desire to receive Holy Communion, it is necessary and indispensable to go to Confession first before receiving Holy Communion. Otherwise one commits a most grave sin of sacrilege, for which Jesus said to St. Bridget, "there does not exist on earth a penalty great enough to punish it sufficiently!"

St. Ambrose said that persons who commit this sacrilege "come into church with a few sins, and leave it burdened with many." St. Cyril wrote even more bluntly: "They who make a sacrilegious Communion receive Satan and Jesus Christ into their hearts—Satan, that they may let him rule, and Jesus Christ, that they may offer Him in sacrifice as a Victim to Satan."

Thus the **Catechism of the Council of Trent** (De Euch., v.i) declares: "As of all the sacred mysteries…none can compare with the…Eucharist, so likewise for no crime is there heavier punishment to be feared from God than for the unholy or irreligious use by the faithful of that which…contains the very Author and Source of holiness."

Instead, Confession made before Holy Communion to render a soul already in the state of sanctifying grace purer and more beautiful, is something precious even if not required. It is precious because it clothes the soul with a more beautiful *"wedding garment"* (CF. MT. 22:12) in which to take its place at the table of the angels. For this reason the most conscientious souls have always made frequent use (at least once a week) of the sacramental cleansing of absolution, even for venial sins.

If you want great purity of soul before receiving Jesus, none is brighter than the purity obtained through a good Confession, where the cleansing Blood of Jesus renders the repentant soul divinely resplendent and lovely. "The soul that receives the Divine Blood becomes beautiful, for it is clothed in a more precious garment, and it appears so resplendently aglow that, if you could see it, you would be tempted to adore it," declared St. Mary Magdalene de' Pazzi.

Holy Communion with Mary

Oh, how much it pleases Jesus to be received by a soul cleansed and clothed with His Divine Blood! And what affectionate delight He takes when such a soul is a chaste virgin! For, remarks St. Albert the Great, "the Eucharist came from the Paradise of Virginity" (namely, Mary); and our Eucharistic Lord does not find such a paradise except in virginity. No one can repeat with the Spouse of the Canticle of Canticles, as can a virgin, at every Holy Communion: *"All mine is my true Love, and I am all His;…He goes out to pasture among the lilies…and addresses His love to me"* (CANT. 2:16–17).

One praiseworthy way of preparing for Holy Communion is to invoke the Immaculate Virgin, to count on her to enable us to receive Jesus with her humility, her purity and her love—praying rather that she herself may come to receive Him in us. This pious practice is much recommended by the saints, in particular St. Louis Grignon de Montfort, St. Peter Eymard, St. Alphonsus de' Liguori, and St. Maximilian Mary Kolbe. "The best preparation for Holy Communion is that which is made with Mary," wrote St. Peter Eymard. A delightful illustration is given by St. Thérèse of Lisieux, picturing her soul as a little three or four-year old girl whose hair and dress were in disarray, ashamed to present herself at the altar rail to receive Jesus. However she appeals to Our Lady, and "immediately," the Saint writes, "the Virgin Mary occupies herself with me. She quickly replaces my dirty dress, ties up my hair with a pretty ribbon and adds a simple flower…. This is enough to make me attractive and enables me to take my place without embarrassment at the Banquet of the angels."

Let us try this method of preparation. We will not be disappointed. We will be able to say what St. Gemma exclaimed in ecstasy, "How beautiful it is to receive Communion with the Mother of Paradise!"

THANKSGIVING AFTER HOLY COMMUNION

The time of thanksgiving after Holy Communion is the most ideal time for an intimate exchange of love with Jesus. Let it be a love of total self-giving, thus returning Jesus' love so wholeheartedly that there is no longer two of us but one, so to speak, in soul and body. Let it be a love that vivifies and unites—He in me and I in Him, so that we may be consumed in the unity and uniqueness of His Love.

"You are my loving prey just as I am the prey of Your immense charity," said St. Gemma to Jesus with tenderness.

St. John wrote, *"Blessed are they that are called to the wedding banquet of the Lamb"* (REV. 19:9). In truth, in Eucharistic Communion rightly received, the soul realizes, in a heavenly, virginal union, a nuptial love for the Spouse, Jesus, to whom the soul can say with the most tender enthusiasm of the Bride in the Canticle of Canticles: *"Let Him kiss me with the kiss of His mouth"* (CANT. 1:1).

Thanksgiving after Holy Communion is a small foretaste, while on earth, of the love which will be experienced in Paradise. In Heaven, in fact, how shall we love Jesus if not by being one with Him eternally? Dear Jesus, sweet Jesus, oh how I ought to thank You for every Holy Communion that You grant me! Was not St. Gemma right in saying that she would thank You in Paradise for the Eucharist more than for anything else? What a miracle of love to be so completely united with You, O Jesus!

Water, yeast, wax

A Father of the Church, St. Cyril of Alexandria, used three analogies to illustrate the union of love with Jesus in Holy Communion: "He who receives Communion is made holy and is divinized in soul and body in the same way that water, set over a fire, begins to boil… Communion works like yeast that has been mixed into dough so that it leavens the whole mass…Just as by melting two candles together, one piece of wax results, so, I think, one who receives the Flesh and Blood of Jesus is by this Communion fused with Him, and the soul discovers that she is in Christ and Christ is in her."

For this reason St. Gemma Galgani used to speak in awed wonder of the Eucharistic union between "Jesus who is All and Gemma who is nothing." In an ecstasy she exclaimed, "What great sweetness there is, O Jesus, in Communion! I want to live in Your embrace and die in Your embrace." And Bl. Contardo Ferrini wrote, "Ah, Holy Communion! Unspeakable heights for a human spirit to reach! What does the world have that equals these pure, heavenly joys, these tastes of eternal glory?"

One may also ponder fruitfully the relation of Holy Communion to the Blessed Trinity. One day St. Mary Magdalene de' Pazzi was kneeling with arms crossed among the novices after Communion. She raised her eyes heavenward and said, "O sisters, if only we would comprehend that while the Eucharistic Species remain within us,

Jesus is there, working in us inseparably with the Father and the Holy Spirit. Therefore, the whole Holy Trinity is present—" She could not finish speaking because she became rapt in ecstasy.

At least a quarter of an hour

The saints chose, when possible, to set no time limit on thanksgiving after Communion, which consequently might last for them at least half an hour. St. Teresa of Jesus told her daughters, "Let us entertain ourselves lovingly with Jesus and not waste the hour that follows Communion. It is an excellent time to deal with God and put before Him the matters that concern our soul. …As we know that the good Jesus remains within us until our natural warmth has dissolved the breadlike qualities, we should take great care not to lose so beautiful an opportunity to treat with Him and lay our needs before Him."

St. Francis of Assisi, St. Juliana Falconieri, St. Catherine, St. Paschal, St. Veronica, St. Joseph of Cupertino, St. Gemma, and many others, used almost always to fall into an ecstasy of love immediately after receiving Holy Communion. As for its duration, only the angels measured the time. So, too, St. Teresa of Avila nearly always went into ecstasy right after receiving Holy Communion, and sometimes it was necessary to carry her away bodily from the communion grille.

St. John of Avila, St. Ignatius of Loyola, and St. Aloysius Gonzaga used to make their thanksgiving on their knees for two hours. St. Mary Magdalene de' Pazzi wanted it to continue without interruption. It was necessary to constrain her so that she might take a little nourishment. "The minutes that follow Communion," the Saint said, "are the most precious we have in our lives. They are the minutes best suited on our part for treating with God, and on His part for communicating His Love to us."

St. Louis Grignion de Montfort used to remain after Holy Mass for thanksgiving at least a half hour, and he would not permit any need or assignment to serve as a reason for omitting it. He said, "I would not give up this hour of thanksgiving even for an hour of Paradise."

Let us, also, resolve to do everything possible so that thanksgiving after Holy Communion last at least fifteen minutes and nothing take precedence over it. These minutes during which Jesus is physically present to our souls and within our bodies are heavenly minutes in no wise to be wasted.

St. Philip and the candles

The Apostle, St. Paul wrote, *"Glorify and bear God in your body"* (1 COR. 6:20). There is no time in which these words, taken literally, apply so well as during the time immediately after receiving Holy Communion. How insensitive, then, for someone to receive Communion and leave church at once as soon as Mass is over, or as soon as he has received Our Lord! We may remember the example of St. Philip Neri, who had two altar boys with lighted candles go to accompany a man who had left the church right after his Communion. What a beautiful lesson! For the sake of good manners, if for no other reason, when a person receives a guest he pauses to give his attention to him and takes interest in him. If this guest is Jesus, then we will only have reason to be sorry that His bodily presence within us scarcely lasts fifteen minutes or a little more. In view of this, St. Joseph Cottolengo personally used to oversee the baking of hosts for Mass and Communion. To the sister assigned to this he gave the following instruction: "Make the hosts thick so that I can linger a long time with Jesus. I do not want the Sacred Species to be quickly consumed."

And why did St. Alphonsus de' Liguori fill the chalice with wine almost to the brim? Only to possess Jesus longer within his body.

Are we not perhaps acting contrary to the example of the saints when we regard our period of thanksgiving as too long and perhaps feel impatient to get it over with? But, oh how we should watch ourselves here! For if it is true that at every Communion Jesus "gives us a hundredfold for the hospitality we show Him," as St. Teresa of Jesus declares, then it is also true that we must answer a hundredfold for neglecting this hospitality. A confrere of St. Pio of Pietrelcina told how one day he went to Confession to the holy friar, and, among other things, confessed to omitting his thanksgiving after Holy Mass because, he said, some ministry impeded him. While St. Pio was lenient in judging the other faults, when he heard him confess this omission, his countenance became stern and he said firmly, "Let us see to it that our being unable is not just being unwilling. I always have to make my thanksgiving; otherwise I pay dearly."

Let us give the matter serious thought and attention. When it comes to something so very precious as this thanksgiving, let us take to heart the Holy Spirit's admonition, *"Let not your share of desired good pass you by"* (ECCLUS. 14:14). Blessed Contardo Ferrini considered preparation for and thanksgiving after Holy Communion so important that every day he would outline the points of reflection, over which he would then linger, all engrossed and happy.

Thanksgiving with Our Lady

There is a special beauty in a thanksgiving made in the company of Our Lady of the Annunciation. Immediately after Holy Communion we too carry Jesus within our souls and bodies, just as the All Holy Mary did at the Annunciation. And we cannot adore and love Jesus better at that moment than by uniting ourselves to the Mother of God, by making ours the same sentiments of adoration and love she entertained for her Divine Son Jesus enclosed within Her immaculate womb.

Our Lady is the heavenly bond that unites Jesus to us; besides, she is the knot of love between Jesus and His creatures. Our Lady, said the holy Curé of Ars, stays always "between Her Son and us." When we pray to Jesus with Her, when we adore Him and love Him with the Heart of Our Lady, our every prayer and our every act of adoration and of love become pure and precious. St. Maximilian Mary Kolbe said that when we entrust something to the Immaculate, she, before presenting it to Jesus, purifies it of every defect—makes it immaculate. The holy Curé of Ars also remarked: "When our hands have touched aromatic substances, these render fragrant all they touch; let us allow our prayers to pass through the hands of Our Lady and she will make them fragrant."

Let us make our thanksgiving after Holy Communion pass through her Immaculate Heart; she will transform it into a most pure canticle of adoration and love.

For this the meditated recitation of the Holy Rosary, especially the joyful mysteries, as many saints teach us, can be helpful.

Who will ever, indeed, be able to know perfectly the Divinity of Jesus, adore Him, love Him and let himself be divinized, as Our Lady was at the message of the Angel? Who will ever be able to bear Jesus alive within himself and remain deeply united to Him in adoration and love as Our Lady did in the Mystery of the Visitation? Who will ever be able to be filled with Jesus, to beget Him, and present Him to others, as did the Virgin Mother in the cave of Bethlehem?

Let us try this. We cannot but gain and benefit in remaining united to Our Lady in order to love Jesus with her heavenly Heart!

Bread to Make Strong and Viaticum for Heaven

In the life of St. Vincent de Paul we read that one day, after having gathered his priests together, he asked them: "Have you celebrated Mass?" "Yes," they all replied. "Then," responded the Saint, "I can now tell you what this entails. You must abandon your country, family, friends and go into exile in a strange land in order to speak about God to the savages and afterwards certainly die, miserably."

Immediately, all these priests, being filled with Jesus, generously offered themselves for that dangerous mission to save souls.

It should go without saying that for everyone Christ in the Eucharist is the true Bread which makes them strong. It is the Nourishment of heroes, the Sustenance of martyrs, and the Comfort to souls in their last agony.

In order to encourage the faithful to receive Holy Communion, St. Robert Bellarmine would preach against the errors of the Protestants in this manner: "The bread of wheat that nourishes our bodies is not prepared with so much labor only to be contemplated; it is made to be eaten. Thus, the Bread of Life, the Bread of the angels, is not offered only for our adoration and homage, but was given to us as food. Let us go, then, and partake of this Food to nourish and fortify our souls."

"I will refresh you"

In the Eucharist, Jesus repeats this affectionate summons to us, mourning and weeping in this vale of tears: *"Come to Me, all you who labor and are heavy burdened, and I will refresh you"* (MT. 21:28). For surely *"the life of man on earth is a warfare"* (JOB 7:1). Moreover, Jesus' followers *"shall suffer persecution"* (cf. 2 TIM. 3:12; MT. 5:10); and it is true that they that are Christ's *"have crucified their flesh with its passions and concupiscences"* (GAL. 6:34), and that we ought to live as dead *"with Christ to the elements of the world"* (COL. 2:20).

It is also true that with Jesus *"I can do all things in Him who strengthens me"* (PHIL. 4:13); for Jesus is *"all"* (cf. JN 1:3; COL. 1:17). In Holy Communion He makes Himself "all mine." Then I can say with the Servant of God Louise M. Claret de la Touche, "What need I fear? He who sustains the world is within me. The Blood of a God circulates within my veins. Have no fear, O my soul. The Lord of the universe has taken you into His arms and desires you to find rest in Him."

In view of this St. Vincent de Paul was able to ask his missionaries, "When you have received Jesus into your hearts, can any sacrifice be impossible for you?" And St. Vincent Ferrer, during the two years he had to suffer in prison as a victim of persecution, abounded with exceeding great joy in all his tribulations (CF. 2 COR. 7:4), because he somehow managed to celebrate Holy Mass every day in spite of the fetters, chains and darkness of the dungeon.

The same courage and joy filled St. Joan of Arc when she was allowed to receive Jesus in the Holy Eucharist before mounting the stake. When Jesus entered her dark prison, the Saint fell on her knees amidst her chains, received Jesus, and was absorbed in deep prayer. As soon as she was bidden to go forth to her death, she rose and began to walk without interrupting her prayer. She mounted the stake and died amid the flames, ever in union with Jesus, who remained in her soul and immolated body.

Strength of the Martyrs

The whole history of the martyrs, from St. Stephen, the proto-martyr, to the angelic martyr, St. Tarcisius, and the martyrs of more recent times, attests to the superhuman strength which the Eucharist bestows in battle against the devil and against all the hellish powers prowling about the world for the ruin of souls (CF. I PET. 5:9).

To cite just one contemporary example, some years ago, in communist China, some nuns were arrested, incarcerated with other prisoners and forbidden even to pray. The guards observed their gestures, their bodily posture, the expressions of their faces and the movements of their lips in order to punish severely any violation. The poor sisters yearned, above all, for one thing: the Eucharist. An old Christian lady offered her services to the bishop to bring secretly to them consecrated Hosts wrapped in a handkerchief. This is the successful stratagem she employed. She presented herself to the prisoners and, in plain view of the guards, she assumed the character of a person mad with rage, spewing a torrent of insults against the nuns; but at the propitious moment she slipped her little bundle to one of the nuns and left the prison, promising the guards that she would return…to mock the sisters!

Remember, finally, the heavenly comfort and aid which Holy Communion brings to the sick, and not merely to their souls, but to their bodies as well, which on occasion are wonderfully healed. For example, with St. Lydwina, St. Thérèse of Lisieux and Bl. Alexandrina da Costa, during the whole time the Sacred Species remained within their bodies, their terrible physical sufferings would marvelously cease. So, too, with St. Lawrence of Brindisi and St. Peter Claver, while they were celebrating Holy Mass, all the pain of the grievous ailments afflicting them would cease.

"Take care of the soul first"

But most consoling of all is the Christian's final Holy Communion, which is called Viaticum; that is, food for the journey from this life to the next. Oh, what great importance the saints attached to our receiving It in good time and with the best dispositions!

When St. Dominic Savio was sent home because of a grave illness, the doctor held out good hopes of his recovery. But the holy youth called his father and said, "Father, it will be a good thing if I deal with the heavenly Doctor. I want to go to Confession and receive Holy Communion."

When St. Anthony Claret's declining health began to cause serious concern, two physicians were called in for advice. Noticing this, the Saint realized the gravity of his illness and said, "I understand; but first let us think about the soul, and then the body." And he wanted to receive the Sacraments at once. After that was done, he sent for the two physicians and told them, "Now do what you want to do."

First the soul, and then the body. Is it possible that we do not appreciate this? Yet, often we are so unthinking that we concern ourselves a great deal about getting in the doctor to tend the sick person, whereas we finally summon the priest only at the last minute when the patient is, perhaps, too far gone to receive the Sacraments with full awareness, or cannot even receive them at all. Oh how foolish, how unwise we are! How shall we render account, if, by failing to call the priest on time, we put a dying person's salvation in jeopardy and deprive him of the support and great help that he could receive in his last moments?

St. Joseph Cafasso was a priest who specialized in assisting the dying (especially those condemned to death). For this he was so much loved by the sick that they would often say: "I would be happy to die, even at this moment, so long as I am assisted by Fr. Cafasso."

However, he would not hesitate to inform the sick, with all prudence and gentleness, of the truth about their condition and of the danger of approaching death. To every sick person, rather, he would immediately advise practicing total abandonment to the will of God to the point of sacrificing one's life. "In this way, if the sickness were to be fatal," the Saint would say, "the sacrifice would already have been offered, and if a healing should occur, the merit would remain."

In addition he would spare no expense when it was a question of bringing Holy Viaticum to the dying. Never. Even in his old age. If someone would tell him, at the foot of a long flight of stairs, to avoid climbing so many steps by sending for a younger priest to bring the Holy Viaticum, the Saint would answer while gazing at the top of the staircase: "I want to climb even higher!"

Holy Viaticum: what a grace!

The Eucharist is the highest guarantee pledging true life to the Christian who dwells in this poor land of exile. "Our bodies," writes St. Gregory of Nyssa, "when united to Christ's Body, attain the beginning of immortality, because they are united to Immortality." When the body's short life is failing, we look to Jesus, who is Eternal Life. He is given to us in Holy Communion in order to be the true and enduring Life of our immortal souls and to be the Resurrection of our mortal bodies: *"He who eats My Flesh and drinks My Blood has life everlasting"* (JN. 6:55). *"He who eats this Bread shall live forever"* (JN. 6:59), because *"I am the Resurrection and the Life"* (JN. 11:25). St. John Chrysostom instructively wrote: "The angels, out of respect for the Divine Eucharist, form a guard of honor around the bodies of the elect who rest in the bosom of the earth."

The Holy Viaticum: what a grace! When St. Teresa of Avila, dying, saw a priest approaching with the Holy Viaticum, to everyone's surprise she rose up unaided from bed, with face ardent and beaming and her whole being extended towards the Holy Host, and she exclaimed ecstatically: "Lord, it's about time that we meet again!"

St. Gerard Majella asked for and received the Holy Viaticum with a piety that was really angelic. When the bell was ringing to announce the arrival of the little procession, the Saint felt moved, became transfigured and exclaimed: "Here He comes to see me, my Lord… See how much graciousness and humility He reserves for me!"

When the holy Curé of Ars was dying and heard the ringing of the bell that announced the arrival of Holy Viaticum, he was moved to tears, and said, "How can we not weep when Jesus is coming for the last time to us with so much love?"

Yes, Jesus in the Holy Eucharist is Love that has become my Food, my strength, my life, my heart's craving. Every time I receive Him, during life or at the time of death, He makes Himself mine in order to make me His.

Yes, He is all mine and I am all His—the one in the other, the one belonging to the other (CF. JN. 6:57). This is the fullness of love for the soul and for the body, on earth and in Heaven.

EVERY DAY WITH HIM

Jesus is in the tabernacle for my sake. He is the Food of my soul. *"My Flesh is food indeed and My Blood is drink indeed"* (JN. 6:56). If I want to nourish myself spiritually and be fully supplied with life, I must receive Him. *"Amen, amen I say to you, unless you eat the Flesh of the Son of Man and drink His Blood, you shall not have life in you"* (JN. 6:54). St. Augustine informs us that the Catholic people in his Diocese of Hippo in Africa called the Eucharist by the word "Life." When they were to go to Holy Communion, they would say, "We are going to Life." What a wonderful way of expressing it!

Bread for the soul and body

To keep my supernatural powers and energies—my supernatural life—in good health, I must nourish them. The Holy Eucharist is exactly what is needed for this, for It is the *"Bread of life"* (JN. 6:35), the *"Bread that has come down from Heaven"* (JN. 6:59), which bestows, replenishes, preserves and increases the spiritual energies of the soul. St. Peter Julian Eymard ventured to say, "Communion is as necessary for us to sustain our Christian vitality as the vision of God is necessary to the angels to maintain their life of glory."

Every day I ought to nourish my soul, just as every day I feed my body in order to give it physical vitality. St. Augustine teaches, "The Eucharist is a daily Bread that we take as a remedy for the frailty we suffer from daily." St. Charles Borromeo supports this: "We must take this Bread as we do ordinary bread when nourishing our bodies." And St. Peter Julian Eymard adds, "Jesus has prepared not just one Host, but One for every day of our life. The Hosts for us are ready. Let us not lose the benefits we can gain by neglecting to receive even One of Them."

Jesus is that Host, that Victim of love, who is so sweet and so healthful to the soul, as to move St. Gemma Galgani to say, "I feel a great need to be strengthened anew by that Food so sweet, which Jesus offers me. This affectionate therapy that Jesus gives me every morning 'unstiffens' me and draws to Him every affection of my heart."

For the saints, daily Communion fulfills an imperative need for Life and Love, corresponding to Jesus' divine desire to give Himself to be every soul's Life and Love. We should not forget that Holy Thursday was the day for which Jesus had *"longed"* (CF. LUKE 22:15). Hence, the holy Curé of Ars said emphatically, "Every consecrated Host is made to burn Itself up with love in a human heart." And St. Thérèse of Lisieux wrote to another sister, "It is not in order to occupy a golden ciborium that Jesus every day comes down from Heaven, but it is to find another Heaven, namely, our soul, in which He takes delight," and when a soul well able to do so does not want to receive Jesus into its heart, "Jesus weeps." "Therefore," continues St. Thérèse, "when the devil cannot enter with sin into a soul's sanctuary, he wants the soul to be at least unoccupied, with no Master, and well removed from Holy Communion." It should surely be evident that we are here concerned with a snare of the devil; for only the devil can be interested in keeping us away from Jesus. May we be on our guard, then. We should try not to fall victim to the devil's deceptions. "Endeavor not to miss any Holy Communion," St. Margaret Mary Alacoque advises: "we can scarcely give our enemy, the devil, greater joy than when we withdraw from Jesus, who takes away the power the enemy has over us."

The dew from Heaven

Daily Communion is a daily wellspring or source of love, of strength, of light, of joy, of courage, of every virtue and every good. *"If anyone thirst, let him come to Me and drink,"* Jesus said (JN. 7:37). He alone is the *"Fountain of water springing up unto life everlasting"* (JN. 4:14). How can there be anyone in the state of sanctifying grace who does not want, or who finds it hard, to go to this divine *"table of the Lord"* (1 COR. 10:21)?

The great Lord Chancellor of England, St. Thomas More, who died a martyr because of his resistance to schism, used to hear Mass every morning and receive Holy Communion. Some friends tried to persuade him that this care was not suitable for a layman heavily engaged in so many affairs of state. "You present all your reasons, and they rather convince me the more that I should receive Holy Communion every day," he said. "My distractions are numerous, and with Jesus I learn to recollect myself. The occasions of offending God are frequent, and I receive strength every day from Him to flee from them. I need light and prudence to manage very difficult affairs, and every day I can consult Jesus in Holy Communion. He is my great Teacher."

Someone once asked the celebrated biologist, Sir Frederick Grant Banting, why he cared so much about daily Communion. "Have you ever reflected," he answered, "what would happen if the dew did not fall every night? No plant would develop. The grass and flowers could not survive the evaporations and the dryness that the day's heat brings in one way or another. Their cycle of energies, their natural renewal, the balance of their lymphatic fluids, the very life of plants requires this dew…." After a pause, he continued: "Now my soul is like a little plant. It is something rather frail that the winds and heat do battle with every day. So it is necessary that every morning I go get my fresh stock of spiritual dew, by going to Holy Communion."

"Those who have little to do," St. Francis de Sales rightly said, "must receive Communion often, since it is not inconvenient for them; the same also goes for those who have much to do, since then they have more need of it." St. Joseph Cottolengo recommended to the physicians of his House of Divine Providence that they hear Mass and go to Communion before undertaking their difficult surgeries. This was because he said, "Medicine is a great science, but God is the great Physician."

St. Joseph Moscati, the famous physician of Naples, would organize his day about this, and go to unbelievable lengths (at the cost of enormous inconvenience, especially in view of the frequent trips he had to make) to avoid missing daily Communion. If on any day it was quite impossible to receive Communion, he had not the courage that day to make his doctor's calls; for he said, "Without Jesus, I do not have enough light to save my poor patients." And how many times he would advise for his patients Confession and Communion as first treatment!

At the cost of great sacrifices

Oh, what ardent love the saints have for daily Holy Communion! And who can properly describe it? St. Joseph of Cupertino, who never failed to receive his beloved Lord every day, eventually informed his brothers in religious life: "You can be sure that I will depart into the next life on the day I cannot receive the *Pecoriello* (the Little Lamb)" as he affectionately and devotedly called the Divine Lamb. And so it came about. One day a severe illness did prevent him from receiving Our Lord in the Eucharist; and that day he died!

When St. Gemma Galgani's father was worried about his daughter's health, he criticized her for setting out too early every morning to go to Mass. His criticism drew this answer from the Saint: "But Father, for me it hurts to keep myself far from Jesus in the Blessed Sacrament."

When St. Catherine of Genoa learned of the interdict under which her city had been placed, with its prohibition of Mass and Holy Communion, she went on foot every day to a remote sanctuary outside Genoa in order to go to Communion. When she was told that she was overdoing things, the Saint replied, "If I had to go miles and miles over burning coals in order to receive Jesus, I would say the way was easy, as if I were walking on a carpet of roses."

This should teach a lesson to us who may have a church within short walking distance, where we can go at our convenience to receive Jesus into our hearts. And even if this should cost us some sacrifice, would it not be worth it?

But there is yet more to this, if we reflect that the saints would have wanted to receive Communion not just once, but several times a day. To a spiritual daughter who in good faith was boasting of her heroic attitude in receiving Holy Communion every day, St. Pio of Pietrelcina once said: "My daughter, if it were possible, I would receive ten Communions a day wholeheartedly!" And on that occasion when a spiritual son accused himself in Confession of having received two Communions on the same morning out of forgetfulness, St. Pio, brightening up, quipped: "Blessed forgetfulness!"

"Full ciborium, empty breadboxes!"

Let us proceed! Let us not require so much prompting to do something so holy as receiving Communion daily, a practice whereby soul and body receive every blessing.

For the soul: St. Cyril of Alexandria, Father and Doctor of the Church, wrote: "If the poison of pride swells up in you, turn to the Eucharist; and that Bread, which is your God humbling and disguising Himself, will teach you humility. If the fever of selfish greed rages in you, feed on this Bread; and you will learn generosity. If the cold wind of selfishness and self-interest saddens you, hasten to the Bread of angels; and charity will come to blossom in your heart. If you feel the itch of intemperance, nourish yourself with the Flesh and Blood of Christ, who practiced heroic self-control during His earthly life; and you will become temperate. If you are lazy and sluggish about spiritual things, strengthen yourself with this Heavenly Food; and you will grow fervent. Lastly, if you feel scorched by the fever of impurity, go to the Banquet of the angels; and the immaculate Flesh of Christ will make you pure and chaste."

When people wanted to know how it came about that St. Charles Borromeo managed to remain chaste and upright in the midst of other youths who were loose and frivolous, they discovered his secret was frequent Holy Communion. It was St. Charles himself who recommended frequent Communion to the young lad Aloysius Gonzaga, later to become the all-angelic Saint with the purity of a lily. Assuredly, the Eucharist proves to be *"the wheat of the elect and the wine which sprouts forth virgins"* (ZACH. 9:17). And St. Philip Neri, a priest thoroughly knowledgeable in the ways of young people, remarked: "Devotion to the Blessed Sacrament and devotion to the Blessed Virgin are not simply the best way, but in fact are the only way to conserve purity. At the age of twenty, nothing but Communion can keep one's heart pure…. Chastity is not possible without the Eucharist." This is so true.

For the body: St. Luke said of Our Lord, *"Power went forth from Him and healed all"* (Lᴋ. 6:19). How many times at Lourdes has this not again and again proved true of Our Savior in the Eucharist? How many bodies have been healed by this kind Lord, enclosed by the white veil of the Host? How many people have there been, suffering from sickness or from poverty, who on receiving the Eucharistic Bread, have also received the bread of health, of strength, of Providence?

One day St. Joseph Cottolengo noticed that a number of patients in his House of Providence had not chosen to receive Holy Communion. The ciborium remained full. Now that same day the pantry ran out of bread for the next meal. The Saint, setting the ciborium on the altar, turned and, movingly, made this pointed comment: "Full ciborium, empty bread boxes!"

This bears out a truth. Jesus is the fullness of Life and Love for my soul. Without Him, I remain empty and dry. With Him, I have endless reserves every day for every good, purity and joy.

Spiritual Communion

Spiritual Communion is the reserve of Eucharistic Life and Love always available for lovers of the Eucharistic Jesus. By means of spiritual Communion, the loving desires of the soul that wants to be united with Jesus, its dear Bridegroom, are satisfied. Spiritual Communion is a union of love between the soul and Jesus in the Host. This union is spiritual but nonetheless real, more real than the union between the soul and the body, "because the soul lives more where it loves than where it lives," says St. John of the Cross.

Faith, love, desire

As is evident, spiritual Communion assumes that we have faith in the Real Presence of Jesus in the tabernacle. It implies that we would like sacramental Communion, and it demands a gratitude for Jesus' gift of this Sacrament. All this is expressed simply and briefly in the formula of St. Alphonsus: "My Jesus, I believe that You are really present in the most Holy Sacrament. I love You above all things, and I desire to possess You within my soul. Since I cannot now receive You sacramentally, come at least spiritually into my heart. *(Pause)* I embrace You as being already there and unite myself wholly to You. Never, never permit me to be separated from You. Amen."

Spiritual Communion, as St. Thomas Aquinas and St. Alphonsus de' Liguori teach, produces effects similar to sacramental Communion according to the dispositions with which it is made, the greater or less earnestness with which Jesus is desired, and the greater or less love with which Jesus is welcomed and given due attention.

A special advantage of spiritual Communion is that we can make it as often as we like—even hundreds of times a day—when we like—even late at night—and wherever we like—even in a desert, or in an airplane.

It is fitting to make a spiritual Communion especially when we are attending Holy Mass and cannot receive Our Lord sacramentally. While the priest is receiving his Holy Communion, our soul should share in it by inviting Jesus into our heart. In this way every Holy Mass we hear is a complete one, with Offertory, sacrificial Consecration, and Holy Communion.

It would indeed be a supreme grace, to be implored with all one's strength, if the desire of the Council of Trent "that all Christians should receive Holy Communion at every Mass they assist at" were in fact soon to be realized in the Church. So doing, anyone able to participate in more Masses every day, will also be able to make more spiritual Communions every day!

The two chalices

Jesus Himself told St. Catherine of Siena in a vision how precious a spiritual Communion is. The Saint was afraid that a spiritual Communion was nothing compared to a sacramental Communion. In the vision, Our Lord held up two chalices, and said, "In this golden chalice I put your sacramental Communions. In this silver chalice I put your spiritual Communions. Both chalices are quite pleasing to Me."

And Jesus once said to St. Margaret Mary Alacoque, the Saint so assiduous in directing her burning desires to Him within the tabernacle: "So dear to Me is a soul's desire to receive Me, that I hasten to it each time it summons Me by its yearnings."

It is not hard to see how much spiritual Communion has been loved by the saints. Spiritual Communion, in part at least, satisfied their ardent desire to be united to their Beloved. Jesus Himself said: *"Abide in Me and I in you"* (JN. 15:4). And spiritual Communion helps us stay united to Jesus, even when we are far from a church. There is no other way to appease the fond yearning consuming the hearts of the saints. *"O God, my whole soul longs for You. As a deer for running water, my whole soul thirsts for God"* (Ps. 41:2).

With the loving sigh of a saint, St. Catherine of Genoa exclaimed, "O dear Spouse (of my soul), I so strongly crave the joy of being with You, that it seems to me that if I were dead, I would come to life in order to receive You in Holy Communion." Blessed Agatha of the Cross felt such an acute yearning to live always united to Jesus in the Eucharist, that she remarked, "If the confessor had not taught me to make a spiritual Communion, it would have been impossible for me to live."

For St. Mary Frances of the Five Wounds as well, spiritual Communion provided the only relief from the acute pain she felt when shut up at home far from her beloved Lord, especially when she was not allowed to receive sacramental Communion. At such times she went out on the terrace of her home and, looking at the church, tearfully sighed, "Happy are they who have received You today in the Blessed Sacrament, O Jesus. Blessed are the walls of the church that guard my Jesus. Blessed are the priests, who are always near Jesus most lovable." Spiritual Communions alone were able to satisfy her a little.

During the day

Here is one of the counsels which St. Pio of Pietrelcina gave to one of his spiritual daughters: "In the course of the day, when it is not permitted you to do otherwise, call on Jesus, even in the midst of all your occupations, with a resigned sigh of the soul and He will come and will remain always united with your soul by means of His grace and His holy love. Fly with your spirit before the tabernacle, when you cannot stand before it bodily, and there pour out the ardent longings of your soul and embrace the Beloved of souls, even more than if you had been permitted to receive Him sacramentally."

Let us, too, profit by this great gift. During the times that we suffer trials or feel abandoned, for example, what can be more valuable to us than the union of our Sacramental Lord by means of spiritual Communion? This holy practice can easily fill our days with acts and sentiments of love, and can make us live in an embrace of love solely conditioned by a renewal so frequent that it seems uninterrupted.

St. Angela Merici was passionately fond of spiritual Communion. Not only did she make it often and exhort others to do it, but she went so far as to make it her daughters' special heritage, because she wanted them ever after to practice it.

What shall we say of St. Francis de Sales? Does not his whole life seem like a chain of spiritual Communions? He resolved to make a spiritual Communion at least every quarter of an hour. So, too, St. Maximilian Mary Kolbe even from his youth. A brief page from the spiritual diary of the Ven. Andrew Beltrami, tells us about what is in fact a little program for a life lived in uninterrupted spiritual Communion with Jesus in the Blessed Sacrament. These are his words: "Wherever I may be I will often think of Jesus in the Blessed Sacrament. I will fix my thoughts on the holy tabernacle—even when I happen to wake up at night—adoring Him from where I am, calling to Jesus in the Blessed Sacrament, offering up to Him the action in which I am engaged. I will install one telegraph cable from my study to the church, another from my bedroom, and a third from our refectory; and as often as I can, I will send messages of love to Jesus in the Blessed Sacrament." What a stream of divine affections must have passed through those precious cables!

Even during the night

The saints were eager to make use of these and similar holy means to provide outlet for their overflowing hearts; for they never felt they had gone far enough in their endeavors to love. "The more I love You, the less I love You," exclaimed St. Frances Xavier Cabrini, "because I would like to love You more, but I cannot. Oh enlarge, enlarge my heart." St. Bernadette eventually begged a fellow sister to wake her up during the night hours when normally she would sleep. Why? "Because I would like to make a spiritual Communion."

When St. Roch of Montpelier spent five years in prison because he had been judged a dangerous vagabond, he prayed continuously, keeping his eyes ever fixed on the window of his cell. The guard asked, "What are you looking at?" The Saint answered, "I am looking at the parish bell tower." It was the reminder of church, of tabernacle, and of the undivided love of the Eucharistic Jesus.

The holy Curé of Ars told his flock: "At the sight of a church tower you can say: Jesus is there, for there a priest has celebrated

Mass." Blessed Louis Guanella, when he was travelling by train on pilgrimage to the various shrines, used always to advise pilgrims to turn their minds and hearts to Jesus every time they saw a church tower from the carriage window, "Every bell tower," he would say, "indicates a church, where there is a tabernacle, where Mass is said, and where Jesus stays."

Let us learn from the saints. They would like to pass on to us some spark of the love burning in their hearts. Let us undertake to make many spiritual Communions, especially during the busiest moments of the day. Then soon the fire of love will enkindle us. For what St. Leonard of Port Maurice assures us of is most consoling: "If you practice the holy exercise of spiritual Communion several times each day, within a month you will see your heart completely changed." Less than a month—clear enough, is it not?

"If I had to go miles and miles over burning coals in order to receive Jesus, I would say the way was easy, as if I were walking on a carpet of roses."

St. Catherine of Genoa

St. Maximilian Mary Kolbe

"I am with you all days, even to the consummation of the world"
(Mt. 28:20).

Chapter IV

Jesus with me

✛ The Real Presence
✛ Visits to Jesus
✛ Jesus I Adore You!
✛ Loving Jesus' House

THE REAL PRESENCE

The Real Presence of Jesus in our tabernacles is a Divine Mystery. During Holy Mass at the moment of the Consecration, when the priest pronounces Jesus' divine words, *"This is My Body.... This is the chalice of My Blood"* (Mt. 26:26–27), the bread and wine become the Body and Blood of Jesus. The substances of bread and of wine are no longer there, because they have been changed— "transubstantiated"—into the Divine Body and Blood of Jesus. The bread and wine keep only their appearances, to express the reality of food and drink, according to Jesus' words, *"My Flesh is real food and My Blood is real drink"* (Jn. 6:56).

Beneath the veil of the Host, therefore, and within the Chalice, is the Divine Person of Jesus with His Body, Blood, Soul and Divinity, who gives Himself to whoever receives Holy Communion, and remains continually in the consecrated Hosts placed in the tabernacle.

The most amazing words

St. Ambrose wrote: "How is the change of bread into the Body of Christ brought about? It is by means of the Consecration. With what words is the Consecration accomplished? With the words of Jesus. When the moment arrives for working this sacred wonder, the priest ceases himself to speak; he speaks in the person of Jesus."

The words of the Consecration are the most wonderful and awesome words that God has given to the Church. They have the power, through the priest, to transform a bit of bread and wine into our crucified God, Jesus! They achieve this wonderful, mysterious feat in virtue of that supreme power surpassing the power of the Seraphim, a power which belongs only to God and is shared by His priests. We should not wonder that there have been holy priests who suffered a great deal when they pronounced those divine words. St. Joseph of Cupertino, and in our time, St. Pio of Pietrelcina, appeared visibly weighed down with distress. Only with difficulty and with pauses did they manage to complete the two formulas of Consecration.

His Father Guardian ventured to ask St. Joseph of Cupertino, "How is it during the entire Mass you pronounce the words so well, but stammer at each syllable of the Consecration?"

The Saint answered, "The most sacred words of the Consecration are like burning coals on my lips. When I pronounce them, I am like someone trying to swallow boiling hot food." It is through these divine words of the Consecration that Jesus is on our altars, in our tabernacles, in the Hosts. But how does all this happen?

"How is it possible," an educated Mohammedan asked a missionary bishop, "that bread and wine should become the Flesh and Blood of Christ?"

The bishop answered, "You were tiny when you were born. You grew big because your body transformed the food you ate into your flesh and blood. If a man's body is able to change bread and wine into flesh and blood, then God can do this far more easily."

The Mohammedan then asked, "How is it possible for Jesus to be wholly and entirely present in a little Host?"

The bishop answered, "Look at the landscape before you and consider how much smaller your eye is in comparison to it. Yet, within your little eye there is an image of this vast countryside. Can God not do in reality, in His Person, what is done in us by way of a likeness or image?"

Then the Mohammedan asked, "How is it possible for the same Body to be present at the same time in all your churches and in all the consecrated Hosts?"

The bishop said, "Nothing is impossible with God—and this answer ought to be enough. But nature also indicates how to answer this question. Let us take a mirror, throw it down crashing on the floor and breaking into pieces. Each piece will multiply the image which the whole mirror previously had reflected but once. So, too, the selfsame Jesus reproduces Himself, not as a mere likeness, but in truth, in every consecrated Host. He is truly present in each One of Them."

They were aware of the Real Presence

Eucharistic wonders are recorded in the lives of St. Rose of Lima, Bl. Angela of Foligno, St. Catherine of Siena, St. Philip Neri, St. Francis Borgia, St. Joseph of Cupertino, and many other saints, who sensibly perceived the Real Presence of Jesus in the tabernacle and in the consecrated Hosts, seeing Jesus with their own eyes or enjoying His indescribable fragrance.

Well known is the episode in the life of St. Anthony of Padua when he once proved the Real Presence to an unbeliever by showing him a hungry mule kneeling before a monstrance containing the Blessed Sacrament, in preference to devouring the basket of oats placed beside the monstrance.

Let us recall what happened to St. Catherine of Siena. One day, a priest who did not believe in the special gifts of the Saint responded to a request to bring Holy Communion to St. Catherine when she was sick, but with a host that was not consecrated. At the entrance of the priest, the Saint did not make a move, as she was accustomed to do, in order to adore the Eucharistic Jesus, but instead, fixed her eyes on the priest and reproved him openly for the deception and for the sin of idolatry in which he wanted her to fall.

The same thing happened to Bl. Anna Maria Taigi who, when receiving Holy Communion, was intentionally given an unconsecrated host. The holy woman instantly realized the deception and experienced a never-ending sadness, which she confided to her confessor.

Equally remarkable was an episode in the life of St. Alphonsus

Maria de' Liguori when he received Holy Communion in his sick-bed. One morning, as soon as he had received the host, he sighed aloud with tears, "What have you done? You have brought me a host without Jesus—an unconsecrated host!" An investigation was undertaken and it was learned that the priest who had celebrated Mass that morning had been so distracted that he had left out everything from the *Memento for the Living* to *the Memento for the Dead* in the Roman Canon, and so had completely omitted the consecration of the bread and wine. The Saint had detected the absence of Our Lord from the unconsecrated host!

Many other episodes taken from the lives of the saints could be mentioned. For instance, cases of exorcism could be recounted where obsessed persons were delivered from the demon by means of the Eucharist. So, too, one might list those great manifestations of faith and love that are the eucharistic congresses and the celebrated eucharistic shrines (such as those at Turin, Lanciano, Siena, Orvieto, and the shrine of St. Peter of Patierno), shrines which to the very present have preserved the testimonials to astonishing events of the past in confirmation of the Real Presence.

The Sanctuary of Lanciano (in Abruzzi, Italy), in particular, is unique of its kind among the world's eucharistic sanctuaries and deserves to be better known throughout the entire world. There the marvelous presence of a Host transformed into live Flesh and preserved in this condition for many centuries can be contemplated. It is a visible miracle which amazes and moves hearts (*see Appendix I*).

"Mystery of faith"

But outweighing all these events and testimonials, is the faith by which the truth of the Real Presence is assured and on which we must base our unwavering certainty that it is so. *"Jesus is the Truth"* (JN. 14:6), and He has left us the Eucharist as a mystery of faith for us to believe with our whole mind and our whole heart.

When the Angelic Doctor, St. Thomas Aquinas, was brought Holy Viaticum, he rose up out of the ashes where he had been laid, got on his knees, and said, "Even if there were to exist a light a thousand times more brilliant than the light of faith, I would not believe with greater certainty that He whom I am about to receive is the Son of the eternal God."

"Mysterium fidei" (Mystery of faith): with these words, Pope Paul VI chose to caption his encyclical on the Eucharist, simply because for divine realities there exist no genuine, certain sources of knowledge higher than theological faith. Precisely on account of this faith, the saints merited to see Jesus in the Host, though they had wanted no further proof than what they had, namely, God's word. Pope Gregory XV declared that St. Teresa of Jesus (whom he canonized) "saw Our Lord Jesus Christ, present in the Host, so distinctly with the eyes of her spirit that she said she did not envy the happy lot of the Blessed who behold the Lord face to face in Heaven." And St. Dominic Savio once wrote in his diary: "To be happy nothing is lacking for me in this world; I lack only the vision in Heaven of that Jesus, whom with the eyes of faith I now see and adore on the altar."

It is with this faith that we ought to approach the Holy Eucharist and keep ourselves in that Divine Presence, loving Jesus in this Sacrament and making others love Him.

Visits to Jesus

With the Real Presence Jesus is in our tabernacles. The same Jesus who was sheltered by Mary Immaculate within Her virginal womb, is, as it were, enclosed in the little cavity formed by the species of a consecrated white Host. The same Jesus who was whipped, crowned with thorns, and crucified as a Victim for the sins of the world, remains in the ciborium as the Host immolated for our salvation.

The same Jesus who rose from the dead and ascended into Heaven, where He is now gloriously reigning at the right hand of the Father, resides on our altars, surrounded by a multitude of countless adoring angels—a sight that Bl. Angela of Foligno beheld in a vision.

Staying with whom one loves

And so, Jesus truly is with us. "Jesus is there!" The holy Curé of Ars could not finish repeating these three words without shedding tears. And St. Peter Julian Eymard exclaimed with joyful fervor, "There Jesus is! Therefore all of us should go visit Him!" And when St. Teresa of Jesus heard someone say, "If only I had lived at the time of Jesus…. If only I had seen Jesus…. If only I had talked with Jesus….," she responded in a lively manner, "But do we not have in the Eucharist the living, true and real Jesus present before us? Why look for more?"

St. Alphonsus Maria de' Liguori comments with customary graciousness: "The sovereigns of the earth do not always grant audience readily; on the contrary, the King of Heaven, hidden under the eucharistic veils, is ready to receive anyone…."

The saints certainly did not look for more. They knew where Jesus was, and they desired no more than the privilege of keeping inseparable watch with Him, both in their affections, and by bodily presence. Being ever with our beloved—is this not one of the primary demands of true love?

Indeed it is, and, therefore, we know that visits to the Blessed Sacrament and Eucharistic Benediction were the secret—yet evident—yearnings of the saints. The time of paying a visit to Jesus is wholly the time of love—a love which will continue in Paradise, since love alone *"does not come to an end"* (I Cor. 13:8). St. Catherine of Genoa made no blunder when she said: "The time I have spent before the tabernacle is the best spent time of my life." But let us consider some examples from the saints.

Ten visits a day

St. Maximilian Mary Kolbe, apostle of the Immaculate, used to make an average of ten visits a day to the Blessed Sacrament—a practice he began as a young student. When the school was in session, during the intervals between class hours, he would hasten to the chapel and thus in the mornings he managed to make five visits to Jesus. During the rest of the day he made five more visits. One of these, during the afternoon walk he always considered a compulsory stop. It was in a church (in Rome) where the Blessed Sacrament was exposed. Similarly, St. Robert Bellarmine during his youth, when on his way to and from school, used to pass a church four times. Thus, four times a day he would stop and pay a visit to Jesus.

How often does it happen that we pass by a church without entering? Are we perhaps that thoughtless and unfeeling? The saints hoped they would find a church along the road they were taking; whereas, we are quite indifferent, even if churches should stand right before us. Venerable J. J. Olier wrote: "When there are two roads which will bring me to some place, I take the one with more churches so as to be nearer the Blessed Sacrament. When I see a place where my Jesus is, I could not be happier, and I say, 'You are here, my God and my All.'"

The angelic youth, St. Stanislaus Kostka, took advantage of every free moment to hurry off to visit Jesus in the Blessed Sacrament. When he simply could not go in person, he would turn to his Guardian Angel and tell him quietly, "My dear Angel, go there for me." And what a truly angelic idea! Why can we not make such a request? Our Guardian Angel would be quite glad to comply. In fact, we could not ask him to do us a nobler and more agreeable favor.

Similarly, the angelic St. Bernadette advised a young fellow sister: "When you pass before a chapel and do not have time to stop for a while, tell your Guardian Angel to carry out your errand to Our

Lord in the tabernacle. He will accomplish it and then still have time to catch up with you."

St. Alphonsus Rodriguez was a doorkeeper. His duties often took him by the chapel door, and then he would never fail at least to look in and give Our Lord a loving glance. When he left the house and when he returned, he always visited Jesus to ask His blessing.

St. Augustine has left us an account about his mother, St. Monica, which tells how, every day, besides attending Mass, she went twice to visit Our Lord, once in the morning and once in the evening. Another holy mother of seven children, Bl. Anna Maria Taigi, used to do the same. And St. Wenceslaus, King of Bohemia, used to travel frequently, day and night, even in the dead of winter, to visit the Blessed Sacrament in churches.

Close to the "hidden Jesus"

Here is another delightful example from a royal house. St. Elizabeth of Hungary, when she was a little girl and used to play about the palace with her companions, would always pick a spot near the chapel so that every now and then, without being noticed, she might stop by the chapel door, kiss the lock, and say to Jesus, "My Jesus, I am playing, but I am not forgetting You. Bless me and my companions. Good-bye." How one loves!

Blessed Francisco, one of the three small shepherds of Fatima, was a little contemplative, who had an ardent love for visiting the Blessed Sacrament. He wanted to go often and stay in church as long as he could in order to be near the tabernacle close to the "hidden Jesus," as he called the Eucharist in his childlike, profound way of speaking. When sickness confined him to bed, he confided to his cousin, Lucia, that his greatest pain was not being able to go visit the "hidden Jesus" so as to bring to Him all his kisses and his love. Here we have a little boy teaching us how to love!

We may add that St. Francis Borgia used to make at least seven visits to the Blessed Sacrament every day. St. Mary Magdalene de' Pazzi used to make thirty-three visits a day at one period of her life. Blessed Mary Fortunata Viti, a humble Benedictine nun of our times, used to do the same. Blessed Agatha of the Cross, a Dominican tertiary, succeeded in making a hundred visits a day, going from her residence to a church. Finally, what shall we say of Bl. Alexandrina da Costa, who, when bedridden for many years, did nothing but fly with her heart to visit all the "holy tabernacles" in the world?

Perhaps these examples astonish us and might strike us as exceptional, even among saints. But that is not the case. Visits to the Blessed Sacrament are acts of faith and love. Whoever has the greater faith and love, feels more strongly the need of being with Jesus. And what did the saints live by if not by faith and love?

Jesus always waits for us

A missionary bishop in India tells of having found a Christian village in which all the inhabitants had constructed their houses with the door facing the church. When they were not able to go to church, they would remain at their own doors and gaze with love at the house of the Lord. Why? Because this is the law of love: to work at achieving union with the one loved.

One day a resourceful catechist said to his young pupils, "If an angel were to come to you from Heaven and tell you, 'Jesus in person is in such and such a house and is waiting for you,' would you not at once leave everything in order to hasten to Him? You would interrupt any amusement or anything else that occupied you; you would count yourself fortunate to be able to make a little sacrifice in order to go and be with Jesus. Now be sure, and do not forget, that Jesus is in the tabernacle, and He is always waiting for you, because He wants to have you near and desires to greatly enrich you with His graces."

How greatly, how highly, have the saints valued the physical presence of "Jesus in person" in the tabernacle and Jesus' desire to have us near Him? So greatly, so highly, as to make St. Francis de Sales say, "We must visit Jesus in the Blessed Sacrament a hundred thousand times a day."

Let us learn from the saints to love our visits to Jesus in the Eucharist. Let us go to Him. Let us remain longer than usual with Him, talking with Him affectionately about what is in our heart. He will fondly look upon us and draw us to His Heart. "When we speak to Jesus with simplicity and with all our heart," said the holy Curé of Ars, "He acts as a mother who holds her child's head with her hands and covers it with kisses, and caresses."

If we do not know how to make visits to the tabernacle which include heart-to-heart talks, we should obtain the beautiful, matchless booklet of St. Alphonsus entitled *Visits to the Blessed Sacrament and to the Blessed Virgin Mary*.

Unforgettable is the only word to describe the way St. Pio of Pietrelcina, every evening, used to read with a tearful voice one of St. Alphonsus' *Visits* during the exposition of the Blessed Sacrament just before the Eucharistic Benediction.

At least one visit a day

Let us begin and be faithful in making at least one visit a day to Our Lord who awaits us anxiously with love. St. John Bosco exhorts: "Never omit the daily visit to the most Blessed Sacrament, be it ever so brief. It is enough if it be constant."

Next, let us try to increase these visits according to our ability. And, if we have no time to make long visits, let us make "Little Visits." Let us enter church whenever we can and kneel down for a few moments before the Blessed Sacrament, saying affectionately, "Jesus, You are here. I adore You. I love You. Come into my heart." A "Little Visit" is something simple and short, but, oh so profitable!

St. John Bosco, with the great heart of a Saint, encourages us still more: "Do you want the Lord to give you many graces? Visit Him often. Do you want Him to give you few graces? Visit Him rarely. Do you want the devil to attack you? Visit Jesus rarely in the Blessed Sacrament. Do you want him to flee from you? Visit Jesus often. Do you want to conquer the devil? Take refuge often at the feet of Jesus. Do you want to be conquered by the devil? Forget about visiting Jesus. My dear ones, the visit to the Blessed Sacrament is an extremely necessary way to conquer the devil. Therefore, go often to visit Jesus and the devil will not come out victorious against you."

Finally, let us always remember these consoling words of St. Alphonsus M. de' Liguori: "You may be sure that of all the moments of your life, the time you spend before the Divine Sacrament will be that which will give you more strength during life and more consolation at the hour of your death and during eternity."

JESUS, I ADORE YOU!

When one loves truly and loves greatly, one begins to adore. Great love and adoration are two distinct things; but, they form a whole. They become adoring love and loving adoration. Jesus in the tabernacle is adored only by those who truly love Him, and He is loved in an eminent manner by whoever adores Him.

The saints, the artists and experts of love, were faithful, ardent adorers of Jesus in the Blessed Sacrament. Importantly, Eucharistic adoration has always been considered the closest likeness we have to the eternal adoration in which will consist the whole of our Paradise. The difference lies only in the veil that hides the vision of that Divine Reality of which faith gives us unwavering certainty.

"At the feet of Jesus"

Adoration of the Blessed Sacrament has been the great passion of the saints. Their adoration lasted hours and hours, sometimes whole days or nights. There *"at Jesus' feet"* like Mary of Bethany (Lk. 10:39), in loving union with Him, absorbed in contemplating Him, they surrendered their hearts in a pure and fragrant offering of adoring love.

Let us listen to St. Peter Julian Eymard who would fervently exclaim: "May I serve as a footstool, O Lord, at Your Eucharistic Throne!" Listen to what Bl. Charles de Foucauld wrote before the tabernacle: "What a tremendous delight, my God! To spend over fifteen hours without having anything else to do but look at You and tell You, 'Lord, I love You!' Oh, what sweet delight…!"

All the saints have been ardent adorers of the Holy Eucharist, from the great Doctors of the Church like St. Thomas Aquinas and St. Bonaventure, to Popes like St. Pius V and St. Pius X, priests like the holy Curé of Ars and St. Peter Julian Eymard, down to humble souls like St. Rita, St. Paschal Baylon, St. Bernadette Soubirous, St. Gerard, St. Dominic Savio, St. Gemma Galgani…, all the saints were ardent adorers of the Eucharist. These chosen ones, whose love was true, kept no count of the hours of fond adoration they spent day and night before Jesus in the tabernacle.

Consider how St. Francis of Assisi spent so much time, often entire nights, before the altar, and remained there so devoutly and humbly that he deeply moved anyone who stopped to watch him. Consider how St. Benedict Labré, called the "poor man of the Forty Hours," spent days in churches in which the Blessed Sacrament was solemnly exposed. For years and years this Saint was seen in Rome making pilgrimages from church to church where the Forty Hours was being held, and remaining there before Jesus, always on his knees absorbed in adoring prayer, motionless for eight hours, even when his friends, the insects, were crawling on him and stinging him all over.

Once when it was proposed to do a portrait of St. Aloysius Gonzaga, a discussion ensued about the posture in which to paint him. Eventually, the Saint was portrayed in adoration before the altar, because Eucharistic adoration was the most distinctive characteristic of his sanctity.

That favored soul of the Sacred Heart, St. Margaret Mary Alacoque, one Holy Thursday, spent fourteen hours without interruption prostrate in adoration. St. Frances Xavier Cabrini, on a feast of the Sacred Heart, remained in adoration twelve continuous hours, absorbed and, as it were, so magnetized to Our Lord in the Eucharist that when a Sister asked her if she had liked the arrangement of flowers and drapings adorning the altar, she answered, "I did not notice them. I only saw one Flower, Jesus, and no other."

After visiting the cathedral in Milan, St. Francis de Sales heard someone ask him, "Your Excellency, did you see what a wealth of marble there is, and how majestic the lines are?" The holy bishop answered, "What do you want me to tell you? Jesus' presence in the tabernacle has my spirit so absorbed, that all the artistic beauty escapes my notice." What a lesson this reply is for us who thoughtlessly go to visit famous churches as though they were museums!

Maximum recollection

A good example of the spirit of recollection during Eucharistic adoration is the striking experience which Bl. Contardo Ferrini, professor at the University of Modena, had. One day, after he entered a church to visit Our Lord, he became so absorbed in adoration, with eyes fixed on the tabernacle, that he took no notice when someone robbed him of the mantle spread over his shoulders. "Not even a bolt of lightning could distract her," it was said of St. Mary Magdalene Postel, because she appeared so recollected and devout when adoring the Blessed Sacrament. On the other hand, once, during adoration, St. Catherine of Siena happened to raise her eyes toward a person passing by. Because of this distraction of an instant the Saint was so afflicted that she wept for some time, exclaiming, "I am a sinner! I am a sinner!"

How is it that we are not ashamed of our behavior in church? Even before Our Lord solemnly exposed we so easily turn about to look to the right and left, and are moved and distracted by any trifle,—and this is what is terrible—without feeling any sorrow or regret. Ah! The delicate, sensitive love of the saints! St. Teresa taught that "in the presence of Jesus in the Holy Sacrament we ought to be like the Blessed in Heaven before the Divine Essence." That is the way the saints have behaved in church. The holy Curé of Ars used to adore Jesus in the Blessed Sacrament with such fervor and recollection that people became convinced he saw Jesus in person with his own eyes. People said the same of St. Vincent de Paul: "He sees Jesus there within (the tabernacle)." And they said the same of St. Peter Julian Eymard, the incomparable apostle of Eucharistic adoration. He found a devout imitator in St. Pio of Pietrelcina, who was enrolled among the Priest-adorers and for forty years kept a little image of St. Peter Julian Eymard on his desk.

Even after death

It is noteworthy that the Lord seems to have singularly favored certain saints by enabling them to perform, after death, an act of adoration to the Blessed Sacrament. Thus, when St. Catherine of Bologna was laid out before the Blessed Sacrament altar a few days after her death, her body rose up to a position of prayerful adoration. During the funeral Mass of St. Paschal Baylon, his eyes opened twice, i.e., at the elevation of the Host and at the elevation of the Chalice, to express his adoration of the Eucharist. When Bl. Matthew Girgenti's body was in the church for his funeral Mass, his hands joined in adoration toward the Eucharist. At Ravello, Bl. Bonaventure of Potenza's body, while being carried past the altar of the Blessed Sacrament, made a devout head-bow to Jesus in the tabernacle.

It is really true that *"Love is stronger than death"* (CANT. 8:6), and that *"He that eats this Bread shall live forever"* (JN 6:59). The Eucharist is Jesus our Love. The Eucharist is Jesus our Life. Adoration of the Blessed Sacrament is a heavenly love which enlivens us and makes us one with Jesus, the Victim, *"always living to make intercession for us"* (HEB. 7:25). We should be mindful that one who adores, makes himself one with Jesus in the Host as Jesus intercedes with the Father for the salvation of the brethren. This is the highest charity toward all men: to obtain for them the kingdom of heaven. And only in Paradise will we see how many souls have been delivered from the gates of Hell by Eucharistic adoration done in reparation by holy persons known and unknown. We must not forget that at Fatima the Angel personally taught the three shepherd children the beautiful Eucharistic prayer of reparation, which we also ought to learn: "O most holy Trinity, Father, Son, and Holy Spirit, I adore You profoundly, and I offer You the most precious Body, Blood, Soul and Divinity of Jesus Christ, present in all the tabernacles of the world, in reparation for the outrages, sacrileges and indifference with which He is offended. And through the infinite merits of His most Sacred Heart and of the Immaculate Heart of Mary, I beg of You the conversion of poor sinners." Eucharistic adoration is an ecstasy of love and it is the most powerful salvific practice in the apostolate of saving souls.

For this reason St. Maximilian Mary Kolbe, the great apostle of Mary, in each of his foundations, before providing even the cells of the friars, wanted the chapel to be constructed first in order to introduce at once perpetual adoration of the Blessed Sacrament (exposed). Once, when he was taking a visitor on a tour of his "City of the Immaculate" in Poland and they had entered the large "Chapel of Adoration," he said to his guest with a gesture toward the Blessed Sacrament, "Our whole life depends on this."

"The better part"

The stigmatized friar of the Gargano, St. Pio of Pietrelcina, to whom crowds flocked from every quarter, after his long daily hours in the confessional, used to spend almost all the remaining day and night before the tabernacle in adoration, keeping company with Our Lady as he recited hundreds of Rosaries.

Once the Bishop of Manfredonia, Msgr. Cesarano, chose St. Pio's friary to make an eight-day retreat. Each night the bishop got up at various times to go to the chapel, and each night despite the different hours, he always found St. Pio in adoration. The great apostle of the Gargano was working throughout the world unseen—and sometimes seen, as in instances of bilocation—while he remained there prostrate before Jesus, with his Rosary in his hands. He used to tell his spiritual children, "When you want to find me, come near the tabernacle."

Bl. James Alberione, another great apostle of our time, expressly placed as the foundation for his entire dynamic work, The Apostolate of the Press (Societá Apostolata Stampa), adoration of the Holy Eucharist. Thus, his Congregation of Pious Disciples of the Divine Master, were given the single, specific vocation of adoring Our Lord solemnly exposed in the Holy Eucharist night and day.

Eucharistic adoration is truly that *"best part"* of which Jesus spoke when chiding Martha for busying herself with *"many things"* that were secondary, overlooking the *"one thing necessary"* chosen by Mary: humble and affectionate adoration (LK. 10:41–42).

What should be the love and zeal, then, that we ought to have for Eucharistic adoration? If it is by Jesus that *"all things subsist"* (COL. 1:17), then, to go to Him, to stay with Him, to unite ourselves with Him means to find, to gain, to possess that by which we and the whole universe exist. "Jesus alone is All; anything else is nothing," said St. Thérèse of Lisieux.

To renounce, then, what is nothing for the sake of what is All, to consume our every resource and ourselves for the sake of Him who is All, rather than for what is nothing—is this not indeed our true wealth and highest wisdom?

This was the way St. Peter Julian Eymard argued when he said, "A good hour of adoration before the most Blessed Sacrament brings about greater good for all than visiting all the marble churches, than venerating all the tombs (of the saints)." This was also evidently the thinking of St. Pio of Pietrelcina when he wrote, "A thousand years of enjoying human glory is not worth even an hour spent sweetly communing with Jesus in the Blessed Sacrament."

What good reason we have for envying the angels, as the saints have done, because angels ceaselessly remain stationed around the tabernacles!

Loving Jesus' House

The Divine Real Presence of Jesus in our tabernacles has always been the object of immense reverence and respect by the saints. Their loving care, so sincere and pure, for the *"things that belong to the Lord"* (1 Cor. 7:32) has been one of the clearest indications of their great love that did not hold back anything, that considered everything to be of great importance, even a simple matter of the prescribed ceremonies, for which St. Teresa and St. Alphonsus declared themselves ready to sacrifice their lives.

Holiness and decorum

And it is from the saints that we must learn to love Jesus, surrounding with affectionate care the holy tabernacles, the altars and the churches, His *"dwelling-place"* (Mk. 11:17). Everything must breathe a sense of decorum, everything must inspire devotion and adoration, even in the little things, even in details. Nothing will ever be too much when it concerns loving and honoring the *"King of Glory"* (Ps. 23:10). Think how of old it was customary, for example, that even the water used for the ablution of priest's fingers during Holy Mass be perfumed.

Furthermore, Jesus chose to institute the Sacrament of Love in a respectable, beautiful place, namely, the Cenacle, a large dining hall with furniture and carpeting (Lᴋ. 22:12). The saints have always shown wholehearted zeal and resourcefulness in seeing to the beauty and tidiness of the house of God, because, as St. Thomas Aquinas teaches, it is necessary to take care first of the real Body of Jesus, then of His Mystical Body.

For example, during his apostolic travels, St. Francis of Assisi used to carry with him, or obtain, a broom to sweep the churches he found dirty. After preaching to the people, he used to address the clergy of the town and fervently urge them to be zealous for the worthy appearance of the Lord's house. He had St. Clare and the Poor Clares prepare sacred linens for altars. In spite of his poverty, he used to obtain and send ciboria, chalices and altar cloths to poor, neglected churches.

When St. Peter Julian Eymard had to begin Eucharistic adoration in a poor abandoned house, the grief he experienced was so great as to make him exclaim even afterwards: "Oh, how dearly it costs me to house Jesus so poorly!"

We learn from the life of St. John Baptist de la Salle that the Saint wanted to see the chapel always clean and duly furnished, with the altar in perfect order and the sanctuary lamp always burning. Dirty altar cloths, torn vestments and tarnished vessels hurt his eyes and much more his heart. He did not consider any expense too great when it came to providing proper worship of Our Lord. St. Paul of the Cross wished altar furnishings and sacred objects to be so spotless that one day he sent back [to the sacristy] two corporals, one after another, because he did not judge them to be clean enough [for Mass].

Prominent among the kings who have loved the Eucharist is St. Wenceslaus, King of Bohemia. With his own hands he tilled the soil, sowed the wheat, harvested it, ground it, and sifted it. Then with the purest flour he made hosts for the Holy Sacrifice. And St. Radegunde, Queen of France, after she had become a humble religious, was happy to be able to grind with her own hands the wheat selected to make the hosts for Holy Mass, and she used to give them free to poor churches. Also noteworthy is St. Vincentia Gerosa, who cared for the grapevines which supplied wine for Holy Mass. With her own hands she cultivated them, pruned them, rejoicing in the thought that these clusters she had grown would become the Blood of Jesus.

With the hands of Our Lady

What shall we say about the delicacy of the saints in regard to the Eucharistic Species? They had uncompromising faith in the Real Presence of Jesus in even the smallest visible fragment of a Host. It suffices merely to have seen St. Pio to realize with what conscientious care he purified the paten and the sacred vessels at the altar. Adoration could be read on his face!

Once when St. Thérèse of Lisieux saw a small Particle of a Host on the paten after Holy Mass, she called the novices, and then carried the paten in procession into the sacristy with a gracious and adoring comportment that was truly angelic. When St. Teresa Margaret found a fragment of a Host on the floor near the altar, she broke into tears because she realized what irreverence might be shown to Jesus; and she knelt in adoration before the Particle until a priest came to take It and put It in the tabernacle.

Once when St. Charles Borromeo was distributing Holy Communion, he inadvertently dropped a Sacred Host from his hand.

The Saint considered himself guilty of grave irreverence to Jesus, and was so afflicted that for four days he had not the courage to celebrate Holy Mass, and, as a penance, he imposed an eight-day fast on himself!

What shall we say of St. Francis Xavier who at times when distributing Holy Communion felt so carried away by a sense of adoration toward Our Lord who was in his hands, that he got on his knees and in that position continued giving Holy Communion? Did that not present a spectacle of faith and love worthy of Heaven?

Something still more beautiful has been the thoughtful care of the saints, who were priests, in handling the Blessed Sacrament. Oh, how they would have liked to have the same virginal hands as the Immaculate! The index fingers and thumbs of St. Conrad of Constance used to shine at night on account of the faith and the love which inspired the use of those fingers to hold the most Sacred Body of Jesus. St. Joseph of Cupertino, the ecstatic saint who flew like an angel, revealed the exquisite delicacy of his love for Jesus when he expressed a desire to have another pair of index fingers and thumbs so that they could be used solely for holding Jesus' most Holy Flesh. At times St. Pio of Pietrelcina quite plainly experienced great difficulty in placing the Sacred Host between his fingers, judging himself unworthy to allow his hands, which bore the stigmata, to have contact with the Host. (What may be the final assessment of the practice, now introduced nearly everywhere, of receiving Communion in the hand rather than on the tongue? By comparison with the saints—so humble, so angelic—do not the reasons adduced in justification seem less than weighty, at times painfully so, and does not the custom itself as often carried out tend to suggest a presumptuous thievery?)

Modesty of women

In view of the decorum of churches and the salvation of souls, the saints were greatly concerned about modesty and decency on the part of the women. A strict insistence on this particular point is a constant in the lives of all the saints, from the Apostle, St. Paul [telling the woman to wear a veil so that she may not need to have her head appear *"as if she were shaven"*: (1 COR. 11:5–6)], to St. John Chrysostom, St. Ambrose, etc., down to St. Pio of Pietrelcina, who would permit no halfway measures, but always insisted on modest dresses clearly below the knees. And how could it be otherwise? St. Leopold of Castelnuovo used to chase women immodestly dressed out of church, calling them "carne da mercato" (flesh for sale). What would he say today, when so many women are abandoning modesty and decency even in church? They are carrying on, even in sacred places, the old diabolical art of seducing men to lust, of which the Holy Spirit warns us (ECCLUS. 9:9). But God's justice will not let such great madness and filth go unpunished. On the contrary, St. Paul says, *"for these things* (the sins of the flesh) *the wrath of God comes upon the children of unbelief"* (COL. 3:6).

In the same way the saints have always exhorted us, by example and by word, to follow the beautiful practice on entering a church, of making the sign of the Cross devoutly with holy water, genuflecting reverently, and before all else adoring Jesus in the Blessed Sacrament in company with the angels and saints who keep watch around the altar. If we stop for prayer, we need to recollect ourselves with care to keep ourselves devout and attentive.

It is also well to draw as near as we can (observing fitting limits) to the altar of the Blessed Sacrament; for Bl. John Duns Scotus has shown that the physical influence of Jesus' most Holy Humanity is more intense, the closer one is to His Body and Blood. (St. Gemma Galgani said that sometimes she could not draw nearer the Blessed Sacrament altar because any closer the fire of love burning in her heart would reach a temperature high enough to set on fire the clothing over her breast!)

The nail on the hat

Whoever saw St. Francis de Sales enter a church, bless himself, genuflect, and pray before the tabernacle, would have to admit that the people were right in saying: "That is how it is being done by the angels and saints in heaven."

Once a prince of the Scottish court told a friend, "If you want to see how the angels in heaven pray, go to church and watch how Queen Margaret prays with her children before the altar." All hasty and distracted people ought to pay serious attention to these words of Bl. Louis Guanella: "We may never turn the church into a hallway, or a courtyard or a street, or a public square." And, in sadness, St. Vincent de Paul exhorted people that before the Blessed Sacrament they avoid making genuflections like marionettes.

May these examples and teachings of the saints not prove fruitless for us.

An amusing episode from the life of St. Philip Neri will help us to recall and keep this resolution.

One day, the Saint immediately stopped a man who was passing hurriedly in front of a church and asked him, "Sir, what is that nail doing there?"

"What nail?" replied the man, amazed.

"Yes, that nail there, on your hat…."

The man removed his hat, looked at it again and again…: there was no nail.

"Excuse me," said St. Philip again with kindness, "there seems to be a nail firmly affixing your hat to your head. That is why you never uncover your head when passing before a church."

The man understood, and from then on he never neglected to take off his hat whenever he passed by a church.

"Happy are you, flowers…"

We find in the Gospel the brief account of a devoted act of love all gracious and fragrant. It is the deed performed by St. Mary Magdalene in the house of Simon the Leper at Bethany, when she approached Jesus with *"an alabaster box of precious ointment and poured it on His head"* (MT. 26:7). To surround our holy tabernacles with an atmosphere of pleasing fragrance is a role we have always entrusted to those lovely, fragrant creatures—the flowers.

St. Alphonsus M. de' Liguori, in a brief strophe, sang thus of his joy and his envy for the flowers that surround the tabernacles with perfume and consume themselves entirely for Jesus: "Happy are you, flowers, who, night and day/ beside my Jesus always stay/ nor ever going away, until/ your whole life through, you shall have always been together!" And also in the care taken to decorate the tabernacles with flowers, the saints have been second to none. When the Archbishop of Turin one day chose to make a visit in the church of the Little House of Providence, he found it so lovely, with the altar adorned and fragrant with flowers, that he asked St. Joseph Cottolengo, "What feast are you celebrating today?" The Saint answered, "We have no feast today; but here in the church it is always a feast day."

St. Francis di Geronimo had the task of growing flowers for the Blessed Sacrament altar, and sometimes he made them grow miraculously so that Jesus would not be left without flowers.

"A flower for Jesus"—a beautiful custom! Let us not deprive ourselves of this gracious gesture of love for Jesus. It may be a small weekly expense, but Jesus will repay it a "hundredfold," and our flowers on the altar will express, by their beauty and fragrance, our loving presence beside Jesus.

But there is still more to be gleaned from this practice and it is reflected in what St. Augustine tells us about a pious custom of his day. After Holy Mass the faithful competed to obtain flowers that had been used on the altar. They would take them home and keep them as relics, because they had been on the altar next to Jesus during His Divine Sacrifice. So, too, St. Jane Frances de Chantal was most diligent in always bringing fresh flowers to Jesus; and as soon as those by the tabernacle began to wilt, she would take them to her cell to keep at the foot of her crucifix. See what one does when one loves!

Let us learn from this and do in like manner.

"Do you want the Lord to give you many graces? Visit Him often. Do you want Him to give you few graces? Visit Him rarely. Do you want the devil to attack you? Visit Jesus rarely in the Blessed Sacrament. Do you want him to flee from you? Visit Jesus often. Do you want to conquer the devil? Take refuge often at the feet of Jesus. Do you want to be conquered by the devil? Forget about visiting Jesus. My dear ones, the Visit to the Blessed Sacrament is an extremely necessary way to conquer the devil. Therefore, go often to visit Jesus and the devil will not come out victorious against you."

—St. John Bosco

St. Augustine, Bishop of Hippo

The Priest is "the man of God"
(2 Tim. 3:17).

Chapter V

The One
who Gives us Jesus

The One who Gives us Jesus

Who is the one who prepares the Holy Eucharist for us and gives Our Lord to us? It is the priest. If there were no priests, there would be no Holy Sacrifice of the Mass, nor Holy Communion, nor the Real Presence of Jesus in the tabernacle.

And who is the priest? He is the *"man of God"* (2 TIM. 3:17). It is God alone who chooses him and calls him from among men for a very special task. *"No man takes the honor to himself; he takes it who is called by God, as Aaron was"* (HEB. 5:4). God sets him apart from everyone else *"to preach the Gospel of God"* (ROM. 1:1). God signs him with a sacred character that will endure forever, making him *"a priest forever"* (HEB. 5:6) and bestowing on him the supernatural powers of the ministerial priesthood so that he is consecrated exclusively for the things of God. The priest, being *"taken from among men, is ordained for men in the things that appertain to God, that he may offer up gifts and sacrifices for sins"* (HEB. 5:1–2).

Virgin, poor, crucified

By his ordination the priest is consecrated in soul and body. He becomes a being totally sacred, likened to the Divine Priest, Jesus. The priest is thereby a true extension of Jesus, sharing in Jesus' vocation and mission. He fills Jesus' role in the most important works of universal redemption, namely, divine worship and the spread of the Gospel. In his own life he is called to reproduce completely Jesus' life—the life of the One who was a virgin, of the One who was poor, of the One who was crucified. It is by thus making himself like Jesus that he is *"minister of Christ Jesus among the Gentiles"* (ROM. 15:16), *"a guide and instructor of souls"* (MT. 28:20).

St. Gregory of Nyssa wrote, "One who yesterday was one of the people, becomes their master, their superior, a teacher of sacred

94

things and leader in the sacred mysteries." This happens by the work of the Holy Spirit; for "it is not a man, nor an angel, nor an archangel, nor any created power, but it is the Holy Spirit which bestows the priesthood on a person" (St. John Chrysostom). The Holy Spirit makes the priest's soul a likeness of Jesus, empowers the priest to fill the role of Jesus so that "the priest at the altar acts in the same Person of Jesus" (St. Cyprian), and "has charge of all of God" (St. John Chrysostom). Who will be astonished, then, if the priestly dignity is declared "heavenly" (Cassian), "divine" (St. Dionysius), "infinite" (St. Ephrem), the "summit of every greatness" (St. Ignatius Martyr), something "lovingly venerated by the very angels" (St. Gregory Nazianzen), so great that "when the priest conducts the Divine Sacrifice, angels station themselves about him and in a choir they chant a hymn of praise in honor of the Victim who is sacrificed" (St. John Chrysostom). And this happens at every Mass!

Respect and veneration

We know that St. Francis of Assisi was unwilling to become a priest because he considered himself unworthy of such a high vocation. He honored priests with a special devotion, considering them his "lords," because in them he saw only "the Son of God." His love for the Eucharist blended with his love for the priest who consecrates and administers the Body and Blood of Jesus. He paid special veneration to the priest's hands, which kneeling he used always to kiss very devoutly. He used even to kiss a priest's feet and even the footprints where a priest had walked.

St. John Bosco exhorts all in this manner: "I urge you to have the highest respect for priests; take off your hats as a sign of reverence when you speak with them or meet them in the street, and kiss their hands respectfully. Keep especially from showing contempt for them in word or deed. Whoever does not respect these sacred ministers should fear a great punishment from the Lord."

The veneration of the priest's consecrated hands, reverently kissed by the faithful, has always existed in the Church. It is noteworthy that during the persecutions of the first centuries, an outrageous cruelty practiced in particular on bishops and priests consisted in cutting off their hands so that they could no longer perform the consecration nor give blessings. Christians used to search out those amputated hands and treating them with spices preserve them as relics.

Kissing the priest's hands is also a delicate expression of faith and love for Jesus whom the priest represents. The more faith and love one has, the more he will venture to kneel before the priest and kiss those "holy and venerable hands" (the Roman Canon), in which Jesus lovingly makes Himself present every day.

"Oh the venerable dignity of the priest," exclaims St. Augustine, "in whose hands the Son of God becomes incarnate as He did in the Virgin's womb!" The holy Curé of Ars said, "We attach great value to objects that are handed down and kept at Loreto, as the holy Virgin's porridge bowl and that of the Child Jesus. But the priest's fingers, which have touched the adorable Body of Jesus Christ, which have been put into the chalice where His Blood was and into the ciborium where His Body was, might anything be more precious than these fingers?" Perhaps we never thought of it before. But it is really so. The examples of the saints warrant this affirmation.

She kissed both hands

In ecstasy the Ven. Catherine Vannini saw angels gather about the priest's hands during Mass and support them at the elevation of the Host and the chalice. We can imagine the reverence and affection with which this Venerable Servant of God used to kiss those hands!

The Queen, St. Hedwig, every morning attended all the Holy Masses that were celebrated in the Chapel of the court, showing herself to be very grateful and reverent toward the priests who had celebrated Holy Mass. She used to offer them hospitality, kiss their hands devoutly, see that they were fed, and show them every honor. She would show deep feeling when exclaiming, "God bless the one who made Jesus come down from Heaven and gave Him to me!"

St. Paschal Baylon was porter in a monastery. Each time a priest arrived, the holy lay brother knelt and reverently kissed both his hands. People said of him—as they did of St. Francis—that "he had devotion for the consecrated hands of priests." He judged that those hands had power to ward off evils and draw down blessings for the one who treated them reverently, since they are hands that Jesus uses.

And was it not edifying to watch St. Pio of Pietrelcina affectionately kiss a priest's hands, sometimes suddenly seizing them unexpectedly? We are impressed, too, by the example of another Servant of God, the priest and Servant of God, Don Dolindo Ruotolo, who would not admit that any priest could refuse "the charity" of letting him kiss his hands.

We know that God has often rewarded this act of veneration by means of true miracles. We read in the life of St. Ambrose, that one day after he had celebrated Holy Mass the Saint was approached by a woman afflicted with paralysis who wanted to kiss his hands. The woman had great faith in those hands that had consecrated the Eucharist; and she was cured at once. Likewise at Benevento a woman who had suffered paralysis for fifteen years asked Pope St. Leo IX to let her drink the water he had used during Holy Mass to wash his fingers. The holy Pontiff granted the request, so humbly made, like that of the Canaanite woman who asked Jesus for *"the crumbs that fell from the table of their master"* (MT. 15:27). And she, too, was instantly healed.

First the priest, then the Angel

The faith of the saints was something that was truly great and produced results. They lived *"by faith"* (ROM. 1:17) and acted on a faith and a love that recognized no limits when treating of Jesus. For them the priest represented nothing more nor less than Jesus. "In priests I see the Son of God," said St. Francis of Assisi. The holy Curé of Ars remarked in a sermon, "Every time I see a priest, I think of Jesus." When she would speak of a priest, St. Mary Magdalene de' Pazzi used to refer to him as "this Jesus." Because of this esteem St. Catherine of Siena and St. Teresa of Avila used to kiss the floor or the ground where a priest had passed. One day St. Veronica Giuliani saw the priest mount the stairway of the monastery to take Holy Communion to the sick. She knelt at the foot of the stairs, and then climbed the steps on her knees, kissing each step and moistening it with tears that her love produced. What examples of love!

The holy Curé of Ars used to say, "If I met a priest and an Angel, I would first pay my respects to the priest, and then to the Angel.... If it were not for the priest, the Passion and Death of Jesus would not be of any help to us.... What good would a chest full of gold be if there were no one to open it? The priest has the key to the heavenly treasures...."

Who causes Jesus to come down in the white Hosts? Who puts Jesus into our tabernacles? Who gives Jesus to our souls? Who purifies our hearts so that we can receive Jesus? It is the priest, only the priest. He is the one *"who serves the tabernacle"* (HEB. 13:10), who has the *"ministry of reconciliation"* (2 COR. 5:18), *"who is for you a minister of Jesus Christ"* (COL. 1:7) and dispenser *"of the mysteries of God"* (1 COR. 4:1). Oh, how many instances could be reported of heroic priests sacrificing themselves in order to give Jesus to their flock! We recount here one instance out of many.

"Farewell till we meet in Paradise"

Some years ago in a parish in Brittany, an old pastor was lying on his deathbed. At that time one of his parishioners was also nearing the end of his life, one of those who had strayed from God and the Church. The pastor was distressed because he could not get up and go to him; so he sent the assistant pastor to him, admonishing him to remind the dying man that once he had promised that he would not die without the Sacraments. The parishioner, hearing this, excused himself with the words, "That promise I made to the pastor, not to you." The assistant pastor could do nothing but leave the dying man, and report his answer to the pastor. The pastor was not discouraged, and though he realized he himself had only a few hours left, he arranged to be carried to the home of the sinner. He was brought into the house, succeeded in hearing the dying man's confession and gave him Our Lord in Holy Communion. Then he said to him, "Farewell till we meet in Paradise!" The courageous pastor was carried back to his rectory on a stretcher. When he arrived, the covers over him were raised, but the priest did not move. He had already died.

The priests are the bearers of "Life," the mediators of salvation between Jesus and souls. Where priests are lacking, the spiritual and moral condition of the people is really frightful; where there is no response to the priestly or missionary vocation, there will be lacking "multipliers" of Jesus, as St. Peter Julian Eymard used to say, and faith weakens or never matures.

It happened on one occasion that a leader of a Japanese tribe asked St. Francis Xavier, immediately after a sermon on the love of God for men: "How come God, if He is so good, as you say he is, has waited so long before making Christianity known to us?" "Do you want to know?" replied the Saint with sadness. "Here is why: God had inspired many Christians to come and announce to you the Good News, but many of them have not wanted to heed His call."

Worthy priests give to every church its stability and fruitfulness. The Venerable Anthony Chevrier said that every true Church has "for its foundation…holy priests; for its columns…holy priests; for its lamp…a holy priest; on its pulpit…a holy priest; at the altar…a holy priest, *alter Christus*!"

Saint or devil

Let us hold the priest in veneration and be grateful to him because he brings us Our Lord. Above all let us pray for the fulfillment of his lofty mission, which is the mission of Jesus: *"As the Father has sent Me, I also send you"* (Jn. 20:21). It is a divine mission which makes the head spin and drives one mad with love when one reflects upon it deeply. The priest is *"likened unto the Son of God"* (Heb. 7:3), and the holy Curé of Ars used to say that "only in Heaven will he be able to measure his greatness. If he were to understand it already here on earth, he would die, not of fright but of love…. After God, the priest is all."

But this sublime grandeur brings an enormous responsibility which weighs upon the weak human nature of the priest, a human nature fully identical with that of every other man. "The priest," said St. Bernard, "by nature is like all other men; by dignity he surpasses every other man on earth; by his conduct he ought to imitate the angels."

A divine calling, a sublime mission, an angelic life, a very high dignity—what immense burdens…all on poor human flesh! "The priesthood is a cross and a martyrdom": an excellent description by that wonderful priest and Bl. Fr. Edward Poppe.

Think of the heavy responsibilities for the salvation of souls laid upon the priest. His task is to bring the faith to non-believers, to convert sinners, to give fervor to the lukewarm, to stimulate the good to become ever better and to encourage the saintly to walk on the heights of perfection.

Now how can he do all this if he is not truly one with Jesus? This is why St. Pio of Pietrelcina used to say, "The priest is either a saint or a devil." He either moves souls to holiness or to ruin. What incalculable ruin does the priest not bring who profanes his vocation by unworthy conduct or worse, who tramples on it, renouncing his consecrated status as one chosen by the Lord (CF. JN 15:16)!

St. John Bosco said that "a priest, either in Paradise or in Hell, never goes alone: with him always go a great number of souls, who are either saved by his holy ministry and good example, or are lost through his negligence in the fulfillment of his duties and by his bad example."

In the canonical proceedings for the canonization of St. John Vianney, we read that the holy Curé shed many tears "as he thought of the ruin of priests who do not correspond to the holiness of their vocation." St. Pio of Pietrelcina described heart-rending visions of the frightful pains Jesus suffered for the guilt of unworthy and unfaithful priests.

Let us pray for them

We know that St. Thérèse of Lisieux, the angelic Carmelite nun, just before she died made her last Holy Communion for this sublime intention: to obtain the return of a stray priest who had renounced his vocation. And we know that this priest died repentant, invoking Jesus.

We know that there are more than a few souls, especially virginal souls, who have offered themselves as victims on behalf of priests. These souls are favored by Jesus in an absolutely singular way. Let us, then, also offer prayers and sacrifice for priests, for those in danger and for those who stand more firmly and securely, for those who are straying and for those who are already advanced in perfection. Unfortunately, people tend much too readily to criticize the defects of priests, while it is rather rare that someone will pray for them.

St. Nicholas of Flüe, a famous Swiss saint, father of a family, bluntly told anyone too ready to point out the faults of priests: "And you, how many times have you prayed for the sanctity of priests? Tell me: what have you done to obtain good vocations for the Church?"

One time, a spiritual daughter of St. Pio of Pietrelcina accused herself in Confession of having criticized some priests for their less than worthy behavior and heard St. Pio forcefully and decisively reply: "Instead of criticizing them, think of praying for them!"

And in particular, every time we see a priest at the altar, let us also pray to Our Lady, in the words of the Venerable Charles Giacinto, "O my dear Lady, lend your heart to that priest so that he can worthily celebrate the Mass." Let us also pray, as St. Thérèse of Lisieux did, so that priests at the altar may touch the most Holy Body of Jesus with the same purity and delicacy as Our Lady. Better yet, rather let us pray that every priest is able to imitate St. Cajetan, who used to prepare to celebrate Mass by uniting himself so closely to Mary Most Holy, that it was said of him, "He celebrates Mass as if he were Her." And, indeed, as Our Lady welcomed Jesus into her arms at Bethlehem, similarly the priest receives Jesus in his hands at Holy Mass. As the Immaculate offered Jesus the Victim on Calvary, similarly the priest offers the Divine Lamb that is sacrificed on the altar. As the Virgin Mother gave Jesus to mankind, similarly the priest gives us Jesus in Holy Communion. Thus St. Bonaventure rightly declares that every priest at the altar ought to be intimately identified with Our Lady; for, since "it was by her that this most Holy Body has been given to us, so by the priest's hands It must be offered." And St. Francis of Assisi said that for all priests Our Lady is the mirror reflecting the sanctity which should be theirs, precisely because of the close proximity between the Incarnation of the Word in Mary's womb and the consecration of the Eucharist in the priest's hands.

Let us also learn in the school of the saints to respect and to venerate priests, to pray for their sanctification and to help them in their very lofty mission.

"We attach great value to objects that are handed down and kept at Loreto, such as the holy Virgin's porridge bowl and that of the Child Jesus. But the priest's fingers, which have touched the adorable Body of Jesus Christ, which have been put into the chalice where His Blood was and into the ciborium where His Body was—might anything be more precious than these fingers?"

—St. John Mary Vianney

Our Lady of the Blessed Sacrament

"…Mary, of whom was born Jesus"
(Mт. 1:16).

Chapter VI

The Bread of
Our Heavenly Mother

❧ The Bread that Our Heavenly Mother gives us

THE BREAD THAT OUR HEAVENLY MOTHER GIVES US

The Eucharist is the Bread of the Mother of God, our Mother. It is Bread made by Mary from the flour of her immaculate flesh, kneaded with her virginal milk. St. Augustine wrote, "Jesus took His Flesh from the flesh of Mary."

"You are my Son"

We know, too, that in the Eucharist, together with the Divinity, are the entire Body and Blood of Jesus taken from the body and blood of the Blessed Virgin. Therefore, at every Holy Communion we receive, it would be quite correct, and a very beautiful thing, to take notice of our holy Mother's sweet and mysterious presence, inseparably and totally united with Jesus in the Host. Jesus is ever Her adored Son. He is Flesh of her flesh and Blood of her blood. If Adam could call Eve when she had been formed from his rib, *"bone of my bone and flesh of my flesh"* (GEN. 2:23), cannot the holy Virgin Mary even more rightly call Jesus "Flesh of my flesh and Blood of my blood"? Taken from the "intact Virgin" as says St. Thomas Aquinas, the Flesh of Jesus is of the maternal flesh of Mary, the Blood of Jesus is of the maternal blood of Mary. Therefore, it will never be possible to separate Jesus from Mary.

For this reason at every Holy Mass celebrated, the Blessed Virgin can in truth say to Jesus in the Host and in the Chalice, *"You are my Son, today I have begotten You"* (CF. PS. 2:7). And St. Augustine correctly teaches us that in the Eucharist "Mary extends and perpetuates her divine Motherhood;" while St. Albert the Great lovingly exhorts: "My soul, if you wish to be intimate with Mary, let yourself be carried between her arms and nourished with her blood…. Let this ineffable, chaste thought accompany you to the Banquet of

God and you will find in the Blood of the Son the nourishment of the Mother."

Many saints and theologians (St. Peter Damian, St. Bernard, St. Bonaventure, St. Bernardine) say that Jesus instituted the Eucharist first for Mary and then through Mary, the universal Mediatrix of all graces, for all of us. So it comes about that from Mary, therefore, Jesus comes to be given to us day by day; and that in Jesus the immaculate flesh and the virginal blood of His most holy Mother are always penetrating our hearts and inebriating our souls. Once in an ecstasy during the celebration of Holy Mass, St. Ignatius of Loyola contemplated the reality at the core of this most consoling truth and for a long time he remained rapt in celestial bliss.

Mary is all in Jesus

Furthermore, if we reflect that Jesus, the Fruit of Mary's immaculate womb, is the whole of Mary's love, of Her sweetness, all of Her intimacy, of Her riches, of Her whole life, then when we receive Him we can do nothing but receive Her as well, who, by bonds of highest love, and by bonds of flesh and blood, forms with Jesus a single alliance of love, one whole, as She is always and inseparably *"leaning upon her Beloved"* (CANT. 8:5). Is it not true that love, and above all divine love, unites and unifies? And after the unity of Persons in the Blessed Trinity, can we conceive a unity more intimate and absorbing than that between Jesus and the Virgin Mary?

Mary's immaculateness, Her virginity, Her tenderness, Her sweetness, Her love, and even the very features of Her heavenly face—all these we find in Jesus; for the most holy humanity assumed by the Word is wholly and only from Mary's humanity, in virtue of the ineffable Mystery of the virginal Conception accomplished by the Holy Spirit, who made Mary Jesus' Mother, consecrating Her a virgin ever intact and resplendent in soul and body.

And so "the Eucharist," writes St. Albert the Great, "produces impulses of angelic love and has the singular capacity of effecting in souls a holy, instinctive tenderness for the Queen of the Angels. She has given us Flesh of Her flesh and Bone of Her bone, and in the Eucharist She continues to give us this sweet, virginal, Heavenly Food."

Finally, just as in the eternal generation of the Word in the bosom of the Trinity, the Father gives Himself wholly to the Son, who is the "Mirror of the Father," so in the temporal generation of the same Word, in the bosom of humanity, the Mother of God gives Herself wholly to the Son, to Her Jesus, "the virginal Flower of the Virgin Mother" (Pius XII). And the Son in His turn gives Himself wholly to the Mother, making Himself similar to Her and making Her "fully godlike," as St. Peter Damian splendidly affirms.

Beside the tabernacle

St. Peter Julian Eymard, that Saint so totally devoted to the Eucharist, declared that already in this world, after Jesus' Ascension into Heaven, the Blessed Virgin "lived a life in and of the Blessed Sacrament"; and thus he liked to call Her "Our Lady of the Blessed Sacrament." And St. Pio of Pietrelcina would sometimes say to his spiritual children, "Do you not see Our Lady always beside the tabernacle?" And how could She fail to be there, She who *stood by the Cross of Jesus* on Calvary (Jn. 19:25)? Therefore, St. Alphonsus Liguori, in his book of devotions, always used to add a visit to the Blessed Virgin Mary to each visit to Jesus in the Holy Eucharist. St. John Bosco said, "I beg you to recommend to everyone, first, adoration of Jesus in the Blessed Sacrament and then reverence for most holy Mary." And St. Maximilian Mary Kolbe recommended that when before Jesus in the Blessed Sacrament, one never fail to remember Mary's presence, invoking Her and uniting ourselves with Her, at the very least by calling Her sweet name to mind.

In the life of the Dominican friar, St. Hyacinth, we read that once in order to avoid a profanation of the Blessed Sacrament, the Saint hastened to the tabernacle to remove the ciborium containing the Sacred Hosts, and take it to a safer place. When, holding Eucharistic Jesus close to his breast, he was about to leave the altar, he heard a voice coming from the statue of the Blessed Virgin next to the altar, saying, "What? Would you take Jesus away without taking Me too?" The Saint halted in surprise. He understood the message, but he did not know how he could manage to carry Mary's statue too. Puzzled, he drew near the statue to see if he could take it with his one free hand. There was no need to strain himself, for the statue became as light as a feather.

There is a precious lesson to be learned from this miracle. When we take Mary along with Jesus, She is no burden and entails no expense, for in a wonderful way they abide in one another (CF. JN 6:57) in a manner divinely sublime.

St. Bernadette Soubirous replied very beautifully to someone who put this tricky question to her: "What would please you more, to receive Holy Communion, or to see Our Lady in the grotto?" The little Saint thought for a minute and then answered, "What a strange question! The two cannot be separated. Jesus and Mary always go together."

Eternal Eucharistic monstrance

Our Lady and the Holy Eucharist are, by the nature of things, united inseparably *"even to the end of the world"* (MT. 28:20). For Mary with Her body and soul is the heavenly *"tabernacle of God"* (REV. 21:3). She is the incorruptible host, *"holy and immaculate"* (EPH. 5:27), who of Herself clothes the Word of God made man. St. Germain came to call Her the "sweet Paradise of God."

Indeed, according to a pious belief, confirmed by the ecstasies and visions of St. Veronica Giuliani and especially those of Bl.

Magdalene Martinengo, in Paradise the Blessed Virgin keeps and will ever keep visible in Her breast a Eucharistic Host. This is for Her an "eternal consolation, an occasion of rejoicing for all the blessed inhabitants of Heaven, and in particular an everlasting joy for all devoted to the Blessed Sacrament." The portrayal of the "Madonna Mediatrice Universale," (Our Lady as Universal Mediatrix), which Mother Speranza recently had painted and which has been placed in the Shrine at Collevalenza, Italy, depicts this belief.

The same theme is often found in monstrances made in centuries past, where Our Lady is depicted with a visible cavity in her breast in which the consecrated Host is put. *"Blessed is the womb that bore Thee!"* cried the woman amid the crowd (Lk. 11:27). Thus, in some of the churches in France, the tabernacle used to be encased in a statue of Our Lady of the Assumption. The significance is quite clear: it is always the Blessed Virgin Mary who gives us Jesus, who is the blessed Fruit of Her virginal womb and the Heart of Her Immaculate Heart.

And She will forever continue to carry Jesus in the Holy Eucharist within Her breast so as to present Him for the joyful contemplation of the saints in Heaven, to whom it is even now given to see His Divine Person in the Eucharistic Species, according to the teaching of the Angelic Doctor, St. Thomas Aquinas.

With Mary in Jesus

It is in the Eucharist, and especially in Holy Communion, that our union with Our Lady becomes a full and loving conformity with Her. With the Host which is Jesus, She, too, enters in us and becomes entirely one with each of us, her children, pouring out her motherly love upon our souls and bodies. The great St. Hilary, Father and Doctor of the Church, wrote beautifully: "The greatest joy that we can give Mary is that of bearing Jesus in the Blessed Sacrament within our breast." Her motherly union with Jesus becomes a union also with whomever is united to Jesus, especially in Holy Communion. And what can give as much joy to one who loves, as union with the person loved? And we—do we not happen to be beloved children of the heavenly Mother?

When we go before Jesus on the altar, we always find Him *"with Mary His Mother,"* as the Magi did at Bethlehem (Mt. 2:11). And Jesus in the Sacred Host, from the altar of our hearts, can repeat to each of us what He said to St. John the Evangelist from the altar of Calvary, *"Behold thy Mother!"* (Jn. 19:27).

With heavenly insight St. Augustine illustrates still better how Mary makes Herself our own and unites Herself to each one of us in Holy Communion. He says: "The Word is the Food of the angels. Men have not the strength to nourish themselves with this Heavenly Food; yet, they have need for it. What is needed is a mother who may eat this super-substantial Bread, transform it into her milk, and in this way feed her poor children. This mother is Mary. She nourishes herself with the Word and transforms Him into the Sacred Humanity. She transforms Him into Flesh and Blood, i.e., into this most sweet milk which is called the Eucharist."

Thus it is quite natural that the great as well as the lesser Marian shrines always foster devotion to the Holy Eucharist, so much so that they can also be called Eucharistic shrines. Lourdes, Fatima, Loreto, Pompei, come to mind. There crowds approach the altar almost endlessly to receive Mary's blessed Fruit. It cannot be otherwise; for there is no bond with Our Lady so close and so sweet, as the one realized in receiving the Holy Eucharist. Indeed, Jesus and Mary "always go together," as St. Bernadette said!

Communion of reparation

Remember, too, that at Fatima Our Lady asked that, together with the holy Rosary, there be above all the Communion of Reparation for all the offenses and outrages which Her Immaculate Heart receives. With great intensity and ardor did Sr. Lucia of Fatima exhort the whole Church to listen to the sorrowful lament of Jesus Himself who showed her the Immaculate Heart of Mary, saying: "Have pity on the Heart of your most Holy Mother wrapped in the thorns which ungrateful men inflict on Her continuously: there is no one to make acts of reparation to remove them from Her."

Jesus Himself, then, searches for loving hearts who desire to console Our Lady by *"welcoming Her into their home,"* as St. John the Evangelist did (Jn. 19:27). We truly welcome Her in the home of our hearts in a manner most intimate and most dear to Her, every time we let Her enter us by receiving Jesus in Holy Communion, and we offer Her the living, true Jesus for Her surpassing comfort and delight. What a great grace it is to be united to Our Lady with Jesus and in Jesus. Did not St. Ambrose desire that all Christians would have "Mary's soul to magnify the Lord and Mary's spirit to exult in God?" This is precisely what is granted us in the noblest way in every Holy Communion. Let us reflect upon this with affection and gratitude and make efforts to imitate St. Peter Julian Eymard, who lived this union with Our Lady so intensely that his companions, in seeing him approach always recollected and amiable, would say among themselves: "Here comes the Virgin!" Or, let us recall the venerable Fr. Placid Baccher, a priest of Naples, whom the people would talk about as being "entirely Our Lady."

Union and resemblance to Our Lady are, therefore, also sublime fruits of the Eucharist that transforms us into Jesus, who is indescribably "all Mary."

"Eat My bread"

One of the old monstrances designed to figure Mary carrying the Holy Eucharist in Her breast has these words inscribed on its base: "O Christian, who come full of faith to receive the Bread of life, eat It worthily, and remember that It was fashioned out of Mary's pure blood." Mary can quite rightfully beckon us and speak to us in the inspired words of Solomon, *"Come and eat my bread, drink the wine I have prepared for you"* (PROV. 9:5). St. Maximilian Mary Kolbe paraphrased this passage when he proposed that all altars of the Blessed Sacrament be surmounted with a statue of the Immaculate Virgin with Her arms extended to invite us all to come eat the Bread that She Herself had made.

In order to receive Holy Communion well, "imagine," St. John Bosco used to say, "that it is no longer the priest but the most holy Madonna Herself who comes to give you the Holy Host." And St. Peter Julian Eymard, with argument deep and brilliant, teaches us that as the Immaculate Conception was the preparation for Our Lady's first Holy Communion, namely, at the Incarnation of the Word, so She continues to be the preparation for every Holy Communion, provided that we ask Her and beg Her that She may cover us with the mantle of Her purity and clothe us with the whiteness and the splendor of Her Immaculate Conception.

A fellow sister one day asked St. Bernadette, "How are you able to remain for so long in thanksgiving after Holy Communion?" The Saint replied, "I consider that it is the holy Virgin who gives me the Baby Jesus. I receive Him. I speak to Him and He speaks to me."

With beautiful metaphor, St. Gregory of Tours said that Mary's immaculate bosom is the heavenly bread box, well-stocked with the Bread of Life that was made in order to feed Her children. *"Blessed is the womb that bore Thee and the breasts that nursed Thee!"* exclaimed a certain woman to Jesus (LK. 11:27). The Immaculate Virgin carried Jesus within Her womb while His Body was being formed from Her own flesh and Her own blood. Thus every time we go to Holy Communion, it should be a pleasure to recall that Jesus in the Blessed Sacrament is the Bread of Life produced from Mary with the flour of Her immaculate flesh and kneaded with Her virginal milk. She has made this for us, Her children. And we realize more fully our brotherhood with one another as we all partake of this delicious and fragrant Bread of our Mother.

St. Peter Julian Eymard gives Benediction

"…And falling down, they adored Him"
(Mt. 2:11).

Chapter VII

Prayers Before
the Blessed Sacrament

✤ Holy Communion
✤ Holy Communion with Mary
✤ Before the Holy Eucharist

Holy Communion

Preparation

Faith—My Lord Jesus Christ, with all my soul I believe that You are really present in the Sacrament of the Altar. I believe it because You have said so—You whom I adore as Supreme Truth. Addressing You in the Sacred Host, I also declare with St. Peter: "You are the Christ, the Son of the living God."

Adoration—I adore You and acknowledge You as my Creator, Lord, Redeemer, and my Supreme and only Good.

Hope—O Lord, I hope that as You have given Yourself wholly to me in this Divine Sacrament, You will exercise Your mercy and grant me the graces I need in order to gain Paradise more easily.

Love—O Lord, I love You with all my heart above all things because You are my infinitely lovable God. Forgive me for having loved You so little up to now. I would like to love You with the ardor of the Seraphim; or better still, with the Heart of Mary Immaculate, Your Mother and mine.

For love of You, O Jesus, I wish to love my neighbor as myself.

Humility—O Lord, I am not worthy to receive You, but only say the word, and my soul shall be healed.

Sorrow—Before approaching You, O Jesus, I ask You once more for the pardon of my sins. You have loved me to the point of dying for me, and I have been so evil, and have offended You countless times. Have mercy on me! Forgive me! By Your grace wipe away even the slightest stain of sin. I wish to approach You with an angelic purity so that I can receive You worthily.

Desire—My God, come into my soul to make it holy. My God, come into my heart to purify it. My God, enter my body to watch over it and do not ever separate me from Your love.

Destroy everything You see in me that is unworthy of Your Presence and can be an obstacle to Your grace and Your love.

> *Remember that within a few minutes Jesus will be within you. This is the most beautiful and greatest moment of your day.*
>
> *Prepare yourself well. Present to Jesus a heart fervent in its love and desire for Him. Be fully aware that you are undeserving of such a great favor, and do not go to Communion with your soul stained by mortal sin, even if you are repentant, because you would then commit a horrible sacrilege.*
>
> *Try to receive Holy Communion during Holy Mass. But if this is not possible, you can equally receive Holy Communion outside Mass, (where Communion services are conducted). Thus you will not miss a day without receiving Jesus.*
>
> *Remember that a fervent Holy Communion 1) preserves and increases sanctifying grace in you, 2) pardons venial sins, 3) protects you from falling into mortal sin, 4) brings you consolation and comfort, with an increase in charity and hope of eternal life.*

Thanksgiving

> *As Jesus is now within you, you have become a living tabernacle. Stay recollected and adore your Lord. Express to Him the fullness of your joy in possessing Him. Open your heart to Him and speak to Him with great confidence, at least for a quarter of an hour.*

Prayer

O Jesus, in the presence of Your infinite love I find myself deeply moved, and, full of gratitude, I can do nothing but repeat, "How grateful I am to You!" But what can I give You, O Lord, in return for Your Gift?

I hear Your sweet voice repeating to me: *"My son, give Me your heart"* (PROV. 23:26). Yes, O Lord, I offer You my heart and my soul. I consecrate to You my whole life. I want to belong entirely to You forever.

To Jesus Crucified

Here I am, O my good and beloved Jesus, I cast myself upon my knees in Your sight, and with the most fervent desire of my soul, I pray and beseech You that You would impress upon my heart lively sentiments of Faith, Hope, and Charity, with true contrition for my sins and a firm purpose of amendment in not offending You again, while with deep love and compassion of soul, I ponder within myself and mentally contemplate Your five most precious Wounds, beginning from what David the Prophet spoke of You, my Jesus: "They have pierced My hands and My feet, they have counted all My bones." *[You can obtain a plenary indulgence, under the normal conditions, by reciting this prayer after communion on any of the Fridays of Lent, cf.* **Handbook of Indulgences***, grant #22.]*

The *Anima Christi*

Soul of Christ, sanctify me. Body of Christ, save me. Blood of Christ, inebriate me. Water from the side of Christ, cleanse me. Passion of Christ, comfort me. O good Jesus, hear me. Do not permit me to be separated from You. From the wicked enemy defend me. At the hour of my death, call me, and bid me to come to You, that with Your saints, I may praise You forever. Amen.

Prayer of St. Bonaventure

Pierce my inmost soul, O most sweet Jesus, with the most sweet and beneficial wound of Your love and with true, sincere, apostolic and most holy charity, so that my soul may suffer and wither with

118

longing because of that same love and the desire for You; may it long for You only and consume itself by that desire for Your dwelling, and may it aspire to be free from the bonds of the flesh and to remain always with You.

Grant that my soul may hunger for You, the Bread of the angels, the Refreshment of holy souls, our daily Bread, that gives us strength and contains in Itself every sweetness, every delight and every pleasing taste. May my heart yearn only to feed upon You, whom the angels desire to look upon, and may my soul be filled with the sweetness of Your savor. May it ever thirst after You, the Fountain of life, the Fountain of wisdom and knowledge, the Fountain of eternal light, the Torrent of every delight, the Wealth of the house of God.

May I always desire ardently for You, search for You, find You, sigh for You, meditate upon You, speak of You, and do all things for the glory of Your Name, with humility and prudence, with love and pleasure, with ease and affection, with perseverance unto the end.

Be always, You alone, my hope, my whole confidence, my wealth, my delight, my joy, my happiness, my rest and my serenity. Be my peace, my sweetness, my perfume, my food, my nourishment, my refuge, my possession. Finally, be my treasure, in whom my mind and my heart may remain fixed, firm and immovably rooted forever. Amen.

Prayer of St. Thomas Aquinas

I give You thanks, O holy Lord, Almighty Father, Eternal God, who has deigned to grant, not through any merits of mine, but out of the condescension of Your great mercy, to nourish me a sinner, Your unworthy servant, with the precious Body and Blood of Your Son, Our Lord Jesus Christ. I pray that this Holy Communion be not to me a condemnation unto punishment, but a saving plea unto forgiveness. May It be unto me the armor of faith and the shield of good purpose. May It bring about the emptying out of my vices and the extinction of all concupiscence and lust, an increase of charity and patience, of humility and obedience, and of all virtues. May It be unto me a strong defense against the snares of all my enemies, visible and invisible, the perfect quieting of all my evil impulses both fleshly and spiritual. May It cause me to firmly cling unto You, the one true God, and may It make my death holy and happy. And I pray You that You would deign to grant in bringing me, a sinner, to that indescribable banquet, where You, with Your Son and the Holy Spirit, are to Your saints true light, fullness of contentment, eternal joy, gladness without alloy, and perfect happiness. I ask this through the same Christ Our Lord. Amen.

Holy Communion with Mary

A Meditation on the Hail Mary

Preparation

O Holy Virgin, I am about to receive Your Jesus. I wish my heart to be like Yours when you became the Mother of the Savior at the moment of the Annunciation of the Angel.

Hail Mary

I greet you, O good Mother. Allow me to unite myself to You to adore Jesus. Lend me Your affections, or better still, adore Him for me as You have adored Him at the moment of His Incarnation in your virginal womb. Hail, O true Body of Jesus, born of the Virgin Mary! I believe, and I adore You.

Full of grace

You, O Mary, were worthy to receive the All-Holy God, for You were full of grace from the first moment of Your life. But I am poor and sinful. My evil ways make me unfit to go to Communion. O my Mother, cover me with Your merits and lead me to Jesus.

The Lord is with thee

The Lord is with You, O most holy Virgin. By Your ardent longing You drew Him down from Heaven into Your Heart. Instill also in my heart an ardent longing and an insatiable hunger for Jesus, so that I can truly say to Him, "Come, O my Jesus, I long for You with the Heart of Mary, Your Mother and mine."

Blessed art thou among women

Blessed are You, O Mary, who have never known the remorse that comes from committing sin; for You are free of every kind of sin and imperfection. But I know I have sinned, and I am not sure that I have been sufficiently sorry. Make me understand the evil of my sins and the goodness of God whom I have offended. I weep for my sins. Present me thus contrite to Your Jesus.

And blessed is the Fruit of thy womb

Ah, good Mother! What a great gift You have given us in giving us our Savior, Jesus! And behold, He wants to come to me to make me an especially beloved child of Your Heart. I go with confidence to receive Him, and I say to Him: "My Jesus, I abandon myself to You. Come to give me strength to serve You faithfully and the hope of enjoying You forever with Your Mother in Heaven."

Jesus

Grant, O Mother, that I experience those sentiments that You have experienced as You lived in Jesus' company, as You called Him by name. I am now about to receive Him. Allow me to be able to say to Him: "Come, O my Jesus. You will find in me the same welcome of love and adoration that You had from Your Mother on earth. I hope that through Her intercession, You will welcome me into Heaven."

Thanksgiving

Holy Mary, Mother of God

O my Mother, how happy I am to be united with Your Jesus! But how do I deserve to have my Lord come to me? O Mary, You who are holy and immaculate, offer Him worthy thanks for me.

You who were the first to hear the heartbeats of Jesus whom I now welcome within me, You who loved Him more than all the saints together, and who lived for Him alone when You were on earth, grant that I may now share Your sentiments of adoration and Your love.

And You, O Jesus, accept the love of Your Mother as though it were my own and do not deny me a tender glance while I also say to You with all my heart, "I love You."

Pray for us sinners

Pray for me, O Mary. At this time unite your prayers to mine. And now that Jesus has come into my heart, willing to grant me all graces, I wish to ask Him above all that I never separate myself from Him by sin. And you, O Mary, preserve me from evil and be my refuge in temptation.

Now

And so, O my dear Mother, I beg for all the graces that are profitable to my soul. Obtain for me this favor: that I be clothed with the virtues of goodness and meekness and that my life be one of spotless purity.

And at the hour of our death

I pray beginning from this very moment, O Jesus, that I may receive You worthily at the time of my death and that my death may be a holy one. I accept it, when and as You shall send it to me—I welcome it in union with Your Sacrifice fulfilled on the Cross. I accept it in order to submit myself to the Divine Will, for the glory of God, for my salvation, and for the salvation of souls.

O Sorrowful Virgin, assist me as you assisted Jesus in His last agony.

"Amen"

"So be it." O Jesus, here is the word that I want to repeat at every instant, both during my youth and throughout my life. May Your will be done always. All that You provide is the best thing for me, and from now on I accept it and give You thanks. Amen.

Before the Holy Eucharist

by St. Alphonsus M. de' Liguori

The Visit to the Blessed Sacrament

My Lord Jesus Christ, who, for the love You bear towards men, remain in this Sacrament night and day, filled with compassion and love, waiting, calling, and welcoming all who come to visit You: I believe that You are present in the Sacrament of the Altar; I adore You from the abyss of my nothingness, and I thank You for all the graces You have given me: particularly for having given me Yourself in this

Sacrament, for having given me Your most Holy Mother Mary as my Advocate, and for having called me to visit You in this church.

I pay reverence to Your most loving Heart today, and this for three purposes; **first**, in thanksgiving for this great Gift; **second**, to make reparation for all the outrages You have received from all Your enemies in this Sacrament; **third**, I intend by this visit to adore You in all the places on earth in which You are present in this Sacrament, and in which You are least honored and most abandoned.

My Jesus, I love You with all my heart.

I repent of having so often displeased Your infinite goodness in the past. I resolve with the help of Your grace not to offend You ever again in the future; and for the present, poor sinner though I be, I consecrate myself wholly to You.

I renounce and surrender to You my whole will, my affections, my desires, and all that belongs to me. From this day forward do whatever You please with me and what belongs to me.

I ask and desire of You alone Your holy love, final perseverance, and the perfect fulfillment of Your will.

I recommend to You the souls in Purgatory, especially those most devoted to the Most Blessed Sacrament and to the Blessed Virgin Mary. I also recommend to You all poor sinners.

Finally, O my beloved Savior, I unite all my affections with the affections of Your most loving Heart, and thus united, I offer them to Your Eternal Father, and I beg Him in Your Name that for love of You He accept them and heed them. Amen.

Spiritual Communion

My Jesus, I believe that You are really present in the Most Blessed Sacrament. I love You above all things, and I desire to possess You within my soul. Since I cannot now receive You sacramentally, come at least spiritually into my heart.

A brief pause is made during which you unite yourself with Jesus.

I embrace You as if You were already there and unite myself wholly to You. Never, never permit me to be separated from You. Amen.

Visit to the Blessed Virgin Mary

O most holy, Immaculate Virgin and my Mother Mary, to You who are the Mother of my Lord, the Queen of the world, the Advocate, the Hope, the Refuge of sinners, I, who am the most miserable of all sinners, have recourse today. I venerate You, O great Queen, and I thank You for all the graces You have bestowed on me until now, especially for having delivered me from Hell, which I have so often deserved. I love You, O most amiable Lady, and because of the love I bear You, I promise to serve You always and do all in my power to make You loved by others. I place in You all my hopes; I confide my salvation to Your care. Accept me as Your servant, and shelter me under Your mantle, O Mother of mercy. And since You are so powerful with God, deliver me from all temptations, or obtain for me the strength to triumph over them until my death.

Of You I ask a perfect love of Jesus Christ. From You I hope to die a good and holy death. O Mary, my Mother, for the love You bear to God, I beg You to help me always, but especially at the last moment of my life. Leave me not, I beseech You, until You see me safe in Heaven, blessing You and singing your mercies for all eternity. Amen. Thus do I hope. So may it be.

Appendix I

The Eucharistic Miracle of Lanciano: Faith, Science, and Popular Piety

All devotees of the Eucharist should visit Lanciano, Italy.

For Lanciano (near Chieti), known to the ancients as Anxanum, is the city where the first Eucharistic miracle in history occurred, one quite exceptional, as the following account will show.

With Bolsena, Siena and Ferrara (to mention a few comparable places), Lanciano is an important name in the religious nomenclature of Italy and of the world. Abruzzi (the region where Lanciano is located), the home of many saints and sanctuaries, takes great pride in this. Here are the facts about this wondrous event.

One morning, twelve centuries ago, a monk of the Order of St. Basil, afflicted by doubts about the Real Presence of Jesus in the Eucharist, had just finished the double Consecration of the bread and wine when he suddenly saw the host change into live Flesh and the wine into living Blood. Astonished and not being able to hide what had taken place, he disclosed the event to the few faithful present. These, almost immediately, went forth to spread the news throughout the city and the surrounding towns.

Thus, in a small city of the Frentanians, in a humble country church dedicated to St. Longinus, the Roman centurion who pierced the side of Christ with a lance, the greatest Eucharistic miracle in history took place as a divine response to a monk's doubts about the Real Presence.

The faithful of Lanciano have continued uninterruptedly since that day to believe in the Miracle, even though circumstances along the centuries have at times tended to diminish the Miracle's fame.

126

Its safekeeping and obscure placement (perhaps out of excessive prudence) were among the principal reasons why this marvelous treasure remained relatively hidden and unknown for such a long time.

Basilian monks (eastern rite) continued to service the church until 1176; thereafter Benedictine monks until 1252 when Bishop Landulf of Chieti entrusted it to the Friars Minor Conventual, who have been there ever since. In 1258 the church was entirely rebuilt in Gothic style and renamed in honor of St. Francis. In 1700 it was remodeled in the present baroque style.

The "Miracle" was first reserved in this church in a chapel situated to the side of the main altar, but in 1636 it was transferred to a side-chapel of the nave. Since 1902 the Holy Relics, kept in an artistic, silver monstrance (of 1713), have been placed at the summit of a new monumental altar. They can, therefore, be admired and venerated by pilgrims close up via a twin set of marble steps.

Today, after a passage of twelve centuries, the Host-Flesh has retained its reddish form. The Blood, contained in an antique crystal chalice and affixed to the base of the monstrance, has coagulated into five irregularly-shaped globules, with a total weight of 16 grams and 505 milligrams. It appears pale and colorless on first glance, but takes on natural hues (resembling the yellow of ochre) when brought near a source of light.

All these circumstances have favored a wider and more rapid diffusion of information about the Miracle itself, culminating in the solemn and universal recognition (examination) of 1971.

Although various ecclesiastical recognitions had been conducted since 1574 by local bishops, during the years 1970–1971 the distinguished Italian scientist, Odoardo Linoli, professor of anatomy and pathological histology, of chemistry and of clinical microscopy, head physician of the hospitals of Arezzo, was engaged to make the first scientific examination of the Flesh and Blood upon the request of the Franciscans in charge of the sanctuary.

The investigation for technical reasons was organized in two phases. The first involved taking some samples from the Holy Relics which Prof. Linoli then brought to his laboratory in Arezzo for testing. The second phase consisted in the presentation of the scientific report made by Professor Linoli on the basis of the completed tests.

The samples were taken on November 18, 1970, in the presence of the Archbishop of Lanciano, Msgr. Perantoni, of the Minister Provincial of the Friars Minor Conventual of Abruzzi and of the entire religious community of the Sanctuary. At 10:15 a.m., His Excellency the Archbishop broke the seals—affixed previously by his predecessor, Msgr. Francis Petrarca, in 1886. The professor took from the Flesh two tiny fragments with a total weight of 20 milligrams and other fragments from the Blood weighing 318 milligrams. Professor Linoli examined the samples over a period of nearly three months. In conducting his analyses he enjoyed the collaboration of a well-known colleague, Roger Bertelli, emeritus professor of human anatomy at the University of Siena.

On March 4, 1971, in the church of the Miracle, before a large audience of scholars, Prof. Linoli made public the results of his analysis. The oral presentation was accompanied by abundant photographic documentation. Here is a summary of his findings:

1) The Blood of the Eucharistic Miracle is real blood and the Flesh is real flesh.

2) The Flesh consists of the muscular tissue from a heart (myocardium).

3) The Flesh and the Blood belong to the human species.

4) The blood type is identical in the Blood and in the Flesh and this very probably indicates that the source is a single person,

although there remains a possibility they could have come from two different persons with identical blood type.

5) In the Blood there were found proteins in the same normal proportions (percentage-wise) as are found in the sero-proteic composition of fresh, normal blood.

6) In the Blood there were also found these minerals: chlorides, phosphorus, magnesium, potassium, sodium in reduced quantity, whereas calcium was found in larger quantity.

The well-known scientist, enlarging on these conclusions, affirmed that—

a) for the Flesh, origin by anatomic dissection from an existing human heart is impossible;

b) no chemical process of preservation was ever employed to conserve the Flesh and the Blood;

c) and, therefore, the preservation of the proteins and the minerals in the Flesh and the Blood is absolutely exceptional, given their exposure to atmospheric and biological agents of decomposition.

The scientific investigation of Prof. Linoli, reported in all the most important medical journals, as well as in a book published by the Sanctuary, has obtained and continues to obtain wide support within the scientific community, nationally and internationally.

In 1973, Prof. Joseph Biondini, an Italian physician and biologist, brought this to the attention of the Administrative Board of the World Health Organization (WHO), of which he was an active member at the time. This Board, in view of the exceptional nature of the report, engaged a team of experts from seven nations to verify the results of Prof. Linoli's analysis, not out of any doubt concerning his honesty and competence, but in view of the extremely important implications of his conclusions for science. After fifteen months of research, carried out singly and in teams with state of the art technology including those of nuclear medicine, the international scientific commission fully confirmed the conclusions of Prof. Linoli. Their report was inserted into the Acts of the WHO, in view of eventual official publication. The aforementioned scientists of the UN have stated categorically that the Eucharistic Miracle of Lanciano is and will remain a "unique case," scientifically unexplainable. The conclusion is hardly a surprise, given the scientific "indemonstrability" of the corresponding "mystery."

The significance of the scientific investigation of the Eucharistic Miracle of Lanciano for theology and spirituality merits a discourse apart. The essential, however, is intuited by the crowds of pilgrims at the Sanctuary.

Face to face with the Miracle, "the profound and respectful sentiments of the popular religious piety" (Paul VI) and the attraction which it exerts over even the most biased are perfectly evident.

A few rough statistics since the latest recognition will serve as an illustration. In the year 1978 there were counted more than 700 pilgrim groups from Italy alone, and in the next year more than a thousand, to which must be added the many individual pilgrims who daily visit the Sanctuary. And the numbers continue to grow. All of Italy, as it were, now seems at home in Lanciano!

In addition there are now large numbers of pilgrims from all over Europe and America. The book: **The Eucharistic Miracle of Lanciano**, has gone through three printings, and in addition to the original Italian, it has been translated into English, French, German, Spanish, Portuguese and Tagalog, the language of the Philippine islands.

In the presence of the Miracle of Lanciano, the great Eucharistic piety of every people, culture and social rank becomes evident, at times explodes. There is no one, even if not physically present, who once aware of this "sign" so perfectly adapted to what it signifies, would not experience a powerful religious call and a deep sense of the divine.

The Eucharistic Miracle of Lanciano, a sublime gift of the Lord to the Church, remains, in accord with the Gospel blessedness of pure faith (CF. JOHN 20:29), an impressive "sign" of things unseen, a stimulating call to make a decisive examination of religious conscience in view of a concrete renewal of life.

On the morning of November 3, 1974, a group of Polish prelates visited the Sanctuary, one of them being Cardinal Wojtyla, now Servant of God, Pope John Paul II. At the end of a long and prayerful visit, of interest in so many ways, he wrote in the visitors' register: "Fac nos tibi semper magis credere, in te spem habere, te diligere." ["Make us ever more believe in You, hope in You, love You"—from the *Adoro Te Devote* of St. Thomas Aquinas, found in Appendix II].

Appendix II

ADDITIONAL EUCHARISTIC PRAYERS AND HYMN

Eucharistic Prayers from Fatima

"O Most Holy Trinity, Father, Son and Holy Spirit, I adore Thee profoundly. I offer Thee the most precious Body, Blood, Soul and Divinity of Our Lord Jesus Christ, present in all the tabernacles of the world, in reparation for the outrages, sacrileges and indifference by which He is offended. By the infinite merits of His Most Sacred Heart and of the Immaculate Heart of Mary, I beg of Thee the conversion of poor sinners."

"O Most Holy Trinity, I adore Thee; My God, my God! I love Thee in the Blessed Sacrament!"

Adoro Te Devote

by St. Thomas Aquinas

Adoro te devote, latens Deitas,
Quæ sub his figuris vere latitas:
Tibi se cor meum totum subjicit,
Quia, te contemplans, totum deficit.

Visus, tactus, gustus, in te fallitur,
Sed auditu solo tuto creditur:
Credo quidquid dixit Dei Filius,
Nil hoc verbo Veritatis verius.

In Cruce latebat sola Deitas,
At hic latet simul et humanitas;
Ambo tamen credens atque confitens,
Peto, quod petivit latro pœnitens.

Plagas, sicut Thomas, non intueor,
Deum tamen meum te confiteor:
Fac me tibi semper magis credere,
In te spem habere, te diligere.

O memoriale mortis Domini,
Panis vivus, vitam præstans homini,
Præsta meæ menti de te vivere,
Et te illi semper dulce sapere.

Pie pellicane, Iesu Domine,
Me immundum munda tuo Sanguine,
Cuius una stilla salvum facere,
Totum mundum quit ab omni scelere.

Iesu, quem velatum nunc aspicio,
Oro, fiat illud, quod tam sitio;
Ut, te revelata cernens facie,
Visu sim beatus tuæ gloriæ. Amen.

Adoro Te Devote

English Version by Father Gerard M. Hopkins, S. J.

Godhead here in hiding, whom I do adore,
Masked by these bare shadows, shape and nothing more,
See, Lord, at Thy service low lies here a heart.
Lost, all lost in wonder at the God Thou art.

Seeing, touching, tasting are in Thee deceived;
How says trusty hearing? That shall be believed;
What God's Son hath told me, take for truth I do;
Truth Himself speaks truly, or there's nothing true.

On the Cross Thy Godhead made no sign to men;
Here Thy very manhood steals from human ken;
Both are my confession, both are my belief,
And I pray the prayer of the dying thief.

I am not like Thomas, wounds I cannot see,
But can plainly call Thee Lord and God as he;
This faith each day deeper by my holding of,
Daily make me harder hope and dearer love.

O Thou our Reminder of Christ crucified,
Living Bread, the Life of us for whom He died;
Lend this life to me then; feed and feast my mind,
There be Thou the sweetness man was meant to find.

(O Jesus like a pelican faithful in distress
Cleanse me in the Blood pouring from Thy Breast;
Which such saving power has one drop of Thine,
All this fallen world to cleanse of every crime.)
Jesu, whom I look at shrouded here below,
I beseech Thee send me what I long for so;
Some day to gaze on Thee face to face in light,
And be blest for ever with Thy glory's sight. Amen.

INDEX

136

Jesus Our Eucharistic Love

How This Book Came to be Yours

This book was published by the Franciscan Friars of the Immaculate, USA, through their apostolate known as "Immaculate *Media*trix." It is being offered for distribution throughout the English speaking world in exchange for an alms to continue their apostolic work.

The Franciscan Friars of the Immaculate [**http://www.marymediatrix.com**] are a reformed community of Franciscans living according to the teachings and example of St. Maximilian Mary Kolbe, Martyr of Auschwitz (1894–1941). Father Stefano M. Manelli, the author of this book founded this community in 1970 at Casa Mariana, Frigento, Italy. They now have houses on every continent. Their religious life is lived according to the Rule of St. Francis of Assisi and the Marian Vow of Unlimited Consecration to the Immaculate Virgin Mary.

If you would like more copies of this book please contact:

For further information:

Academy of the Immaculate
124 North Forke
Advance, NC 27006
Tel. /Fax: (336) 940-5976
E-mail: mimike@pipeline.com
or
Franciscans of the Immaculate,
P.O. Box 3003
New Bedford, MA 02741-3003,
Tel. # (508) 996-8274, FAX (508) 996-8296,
E-mail: ffi@marymediatrix.com
Website: www.marymediatrix.com

The Academy of the Immaculate Books

Obviously there is a need for good, solid devotional books on Marian Shrines and Saints outstanding in their love for the Blessed Mother and the Eucharistic Jesus. The Franciscans of the Immaculate are attempting to meet this need and flood the book market with readable inspirational books at a reasonable cost.

All Generations Shall Call Me Blessed

by Stefano Manelli, F.I. A scholarly easy to read book tracing Mary's role in the Old Testament through prophecies, figures, and symbols to Mary's presence in the New Testament. A concise exposition which shows clearly Mary's place in the economy of Salvation.

Totus Tuus *by Msgr. Arthur Burton Calkins* Provides a thorough examination of Pope John Paul II's thoughts on total consecration or entrustment to Our Lady based on the historic, theological and scriptural evidence. Vital in clearing away some misunderstandings about entrustment and consecration.

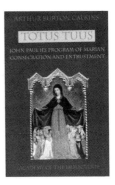

140

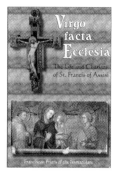

Virgo Facta Ecclesia *by Franciscans of the Immaculate* is made up of two parts: the first a biography on St. Francis of Assisi and the second part on the Marian character of the Franciscan Order based on its long Marian tradition, from St. Francis to St. Maximilian Kolbe.

Not Made by Hands *by Thomas Sennott* An excellent resource book covering the two most controversial images in existence: the Holy Image of Our Lady of Guadalupe on the tilma of Juan Diego and the Sacred Image of the Crucified on the Shroud of Turin, giving scientific evidence for their authenticity and exposing the fraudulent carbon 14 test.

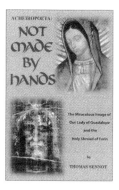

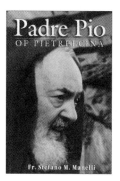

Padre Pio of Pietrelcina *by Fr, Stefano Manelli, F.I.* This 144 page popular life of Padre Pio is packed with details about his life, spirituality, and charisms, by one who knew the Padre intimately. The author turned to Padre Pio for guidance in establishing a new Community, the Franciscans of the Immaculate.

Come Follow Me *by Fr. Stefano Manelli, F.I.* A book directed to any young person contemplating a Religious vocation. Informative, with many inspiring illustrations and words from the lives and writings of the Saints on the challenging vocation of total dedication in the following of Christ and His Immaculate Mother through the three vows of religion.

Mary at the Foot of the Cross With so much attention focused today on whether the Church should define the long-standing traditional teaching of the Church that Mary is the Mediatrix of all Graces, this symposium on Marian Coredemption addresses supporting evidences for its definition. The week-long symposium, which took place at Ratcliffe College in England, had 18 conferences beside a prayerful "retreat" which included Eucharistic Adoration, Rosary and the Little Hours of the Office. Many 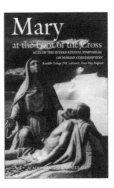 well-known Mariologists gave papers, such as: Bishop Paul Hnilica, Fr. Bertrand De Margerie, S.J., Dr. Mark Miravalle, Fr. Stefano Manelli, F.I., Fr. Aidan Nichols, O.P., Mother Francesca Perillo, F.I., Msgr. Arthur Calkins, and Fr. Peter Damian Mary Fehlner, F.I., who was the moderator, introducing the speakers.

Devotion to Our Lady *by Fr. Stefano M. Manelli, F.I.* This book is a must for all those who desire to know the beauty and value of Marian devotion and want to increase their fervent love towards their heavenly Mother. Since it draws abundantly from the examples and writings of the Saints, it offers the devotee a very concrete and practical aid for living out a truly Marian life.

Who is Mary? *Fr. Gabriel M. Pellettieri, F.I.* This book is a concise Marian catechism presented in a question/answer format. In this little work of love and scholarship the sweet mystery of Mary is unveiled in all its beauty and simplicity. It is a very helpful resource both for those who want to know the truth about Mary and those who want to instruct others.

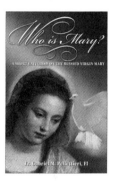

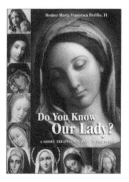

Do You Know Our Lady? *Mother Maria Francesca Perillo, F.I.* This excellent, handy treatise (125 pages) covers the rich and profound references to Mary, as prefigured in the Old Testament women and prophecies and as found in the New Testament, at the momentous events of Salvation History, from the Annunciation to Pentecost. In keeping with the Church's long tradition of placing Mary's role in the center, beside her Divine Son, through legitimate Scriptural interpretation, the author demonstrates a number of times how Scripture supports Mary's role as Mediatrix of All Graces. The coverage of the historicity of the Infancy Narratives in the Gospel is particularly good in answering Scriptural scholars who attempt to discredit what the Church has always held as historically true.

Saints and Marian Shrine Series

Edited by Bro. Francis Mary, F.I.

A Handbook on Guadalupe This well researched book on Guadalupe contains 40 topical chapters by leading experts on Guadalupe with new insights and the latest scientific findings. A number of chapters deal with Our Lady's role as the patroness of the pro-life movement. Well illustrated.

St. Thérèse: Doctor of the Little Way A compendium of 32 chapters covering many unique facets about the latest Doctor of the Church by 23 authors including Fr. John Hardon, S.J., Msgr. Vernon Johnson, Sister Marie of the Trinity, OCD, and Stephanè Piat. The 174 page book is well illustrated.

Padre Pio — The Wonder Worker The latest on this popular saint of our times including the two inspirational homilies given by Pope John Paul II during the beatification celebration in Rome. The first part of the book is a short biography. The second is on his spirituality, charisms, apostolate of the confessional, and his great works of charity.

Marian Shrines of France On the four major Marian shrines and apparitions of France during the 19th century: Our Lady at Rue du Bac (Paris), La Salette, Lourdes and Pointmain. Shows how already in the 19th century Our Lady checkmated our secular, Godless 20th century introducing the present Age of Mary. Well illustrated.

Marian Shrines of Italy The latest in the series of "Marian Saints and Shrines," with 36 pages of colorful illustrations on over thirty of the 1500 Marian shrines in Italy. The book covers that topic with an underlying theme of the intimate and vital relationship between Mary and the Church. This is especially apparent in Catholic Italy, where the center of the Catholic Faith is found in Rome.

Kolbe - Saint of the Immaculata Of all the books in the *Marian Saints and Shrines* series, this one is the most controversial and thus the most needed in order to do justice to the Saint, whom Pope John Paul II spoke of as "the Saint of our difficult century [twentieth]." Is it true, as reported in a PBS documentary, that the Saint was anti-Semitic? What is the reason behind misrepresenting this great modern day Saint? Is a famous Mariologist right in accusing the Saint of being in error by holding that Mary is the Mediatrix of all Graces? The book has over 35 chapters by over ten authors, giving an in-depth view of one of the greatest Marian Saints of all times.

THE ACADEMY OF THE IMMACULATE

The Academy of the Immaculate, founded in 1992, is inspired by and based on a project of St. Maximilian M. Kolbe (never realized by the Saint because of his death by martyrdom at the age of 47, August 14, 1941). Among its goals the Academy seeks to promote at every level the study of the Mystery of the Immaculate Conception and the universal maternal mediation of the Virgin Mother of God, and to sponsor publication and dissemination of the fruits of this research in every way possible.

The Academy of the Immaculate is a non-profit religious-charitable organization of the Roman Catholic Church, incorporated under the laws of the Commonwealth of Massachusetts, with its central office at Our Lady's Chapel, POB 3003, New Bedford, MA 02741-3003.

NOTES

NOTES